CW00555035

Teacher's Handbook

STAGES 9–16

Compiled by
Catherine Baker, Thelma Page
and Charlotte Raby

OXFORD
UNIVERSITY PRESS

OXFORD
UNIVERSITY PRESS

Great Clarendon Street, Oxford OX2 6DP

Oxford University Press is a department of the University of Oxford.
It furthers the University's objective of excellence in research, scholarship,
and education by publishing worldwide in

Oxford   New York

Auckland Cape Town Dar es Salaam Hong Kong Karachi
Kuala Lumpur Madrid Melbourne Mexico City Nairobi
New Delhi Shanghai Taipei Toronto

With offices in

Argentina Austria Brazil Chile Czech Republic France Greece
Guatemala Hungary Italy Japan Poland Portugal Singapore
South Korea Switzerland Thailand Turkey Ukraine Vietnam

Oxford is a registered trade mark of Oxford University Press
in the UK and in certain other countries

© Oxford University Press 2010

The moral rights of the author have been asserted

Database right Oxford University Press (maker)

First published 2010

Written by Catherine Baker, Thelma Page and Charlotte Raby

All rights reserved. No part of this publication may be reproduced,
stored in a retrieval system, or transmitted, in any form or by any means,
without the prior permission in writing of Oxford University Press,
or as expressly permitted by law, or under terms agreed with the appropriate
reprographics rights organization. Enquiries concerning reproduction
outside the scope of the above should be sent to the Rights Department,
Oxford University Press, at the address above

You must not circulate this book in any other binding or cover
and you must impose this same condition on any acquirer

British Library Cataloguing in Publication Data

Data available

ISBN: 978-0-19-918053-0

9 10 8

Acknowledgements

Cover artwork: Vakhrushev Pavel/Shutterstock, Chris Smedley,
Jason Loo, Andrés Martínez Ricci, Martin Remphry and OUP

Inside illustrations by OUP

Page make-up by Thomson Digital

With thanks to the following schools for providing the case studies included within this handbook:

Hangleton Junior School, Brighton & Hove
Hempland Primary School, Heworth, York
Ince Church of England Primary School, Higher Ince, Wigan
St Tudy Church of England Primary School, Bodmin, Cornwall

To ensure that curriculum guidance is not misinterpreted, references to the National Curriculum
Assessment Guidelines (pages 36–63) and Framework Objectives (pages 69–84) have been taken from
the curriculum guidance provided by the following organisations:

The Department for Children, Schools and Families
The National Strategies
Assessment Guidelines
© Crown Copyright 1997–2009
http://nationalstrategies.standards.dcsf.gov.uk/node/20234

The Department for Children, Schools and Families
The National Strategies
Primary Framework Objectives
© Crown Copyright 1997–2009
http://www.nationalstrategies.standards.dcsf.gov.uk/node/110237

Please be aware that website addresses are liable to change

Printed in Great Britain by Bell & Bain Ltd., Glasgow

Paper used in the production of this book is a natural, recyclable product
made from wood grown in sustainable forests. The manufacturing process
conforms to the environmental regulations of the country of origin.

P references relate to primary year groups in Northern Ireland

Contents

What is TreeTops?

A core resource for teaching literacy with juniors

TreeTops offers a specially designed suite of resources to cover every aspect of literacy teaching. At the heart of TreeTops is a wealth of motivating fiction and non-fiction books, and the programme also includes dedicated resources to help you teach comprehension and writing. Children's literacy development is enhanced with plays, graphic novels and motivating on-screen resources. With such a wide range of resources at your disposal, and dedicated teaching support for each component, you can confidently use TreeTops as your core resource for literacy teaching.

TreeTops Fiction

- A wide range of funny and exciting stories by well-known authors
- Covers the full range of fiction genres
- Levelled by stages, not ages – so you can find books at the appropriate level for all your junior readers

TreeTops Non-fiction

- Fascinating topics and great photography for real child-appeal
- Covers the full range of non-fiction genres
- Carefully levelled for gradual progression – motivating and stretching both able and reluctant readers

TreeTops True Stories

- Fascinating narrative non-fiction, including biographies of famous people as diverse as Nelson Mandela, and Blackbeard the pirate, and historical recounts of subjects such as the Black Death and the discovery of Tutankhamun's tomb

TreeTops Myths and Legends

- 24 books containing 70 traditional stories from around the world, illustrated with stunning vibrant images in a range of styles
- Allows children to experience the action, drama, humour and depth of the original stories and provides them with the opportunity to learn more about different cultures

TreeTops Playscripts

- Fun playscript versions of selected TreeTops stories
- Ideal for motivating reluctant readers and encouraging fluency
- Useful for speaking and listening and drama activities

TreeTops!

A flexible resource bank to meet all your literacy needs

Whether you are using TreeTops as your core literacy resource or not, it provides an essential resource bank to help you meet children's developing needs throughout the juniors. You can pick from inspiring fiction and non-fiction, adaptations of classic texts, playscripts, comprehension and writing resources, and use them either on their own or to supplement your other teaching resources.

TreeTops Comprehension

- Teaches comprehension skills and strategies through motivating, levelled texts that children can both read and enjoy
- Whiteboard resources to help structure successful whole-class teaching sessions
- *Pupil's Books* for group and independent work, giving plenty of opportunities to practise key skills

TreeTops Storywriter

- Shows children how to plan, structure and write good stories in five easy steps
- Whiteboard resources and *Pupil Books* work together for successful whole-class and individual work
- Fully supports the Talk for Writing approach to teaching writing skills

TreeTops Talking Stories

- Interactive electronic versions of selected books, for use on the whiteboard or small screen
- Reinforces comprehension and encourages reading fluency

TreeTops Graphic Novels

- Beautifully designed and illustrated graphic novels with particular appeal for less confident readers
- Includes exciting stories from around the world and set in different historical periods, to support work across the curriculum

TreeTops Classics

- 24 motivating and accessible versions of classic texts, carefully levelled for juniors to enjoy
- Includes well-loved children's stories such as *The Jungle Book* and *Black Beauty*, as well as timeless classics such as *Frankenstein, Jane Eyre* and *Macbeth*

TreeTops component chart

The chart below shows the main components available at each Stage of TreeTops. For more detailed information on individual titles, please see the charts on pages 85–93 which give key genre and levelling information for each title.

Stage	TreeTops Fiction	TreeTops Non-fiction	TreeTops True Stories	TreeTops Classics	TreeTops Graphic Novels	TreeTops Myths and Legends	TreeTops Playscripts	TreeTops Talking Stories	TreeTops Comprehension	TreeTops Storywriter
9	12 books	6 books				3 books				
10	18 books	12 books				3 books	2 books	3 books	Year 3/P4	Year 3/P4
11	18 books	12 books	Pack 1: 6 books			3 books	2 books	3 books	CD-ROM Pupils' Book Teacher's Guide	CD-ROM Pupil Book Teacher's Guide
12	24 books	12 books				3 books	2 books		Year 4/P5	Year 4/P5
13	18 books	6 books			6 books	3 books	2 books		CD-ROM Pupils' Book Teacher's Guide	CD-ROM Pupil Book Teacher's Guide
14	12 books	6 books	Pack 2: 6 books	6 books	6 books	3 books	2 books		Year 5/P6 CD-ROM Pupils' Book Teacher's Guide	Year 5/P6 CD-ROM Pupil Book Teacher's Guide
15	12 books	6 books		6 books	6 books	3 books			Year 6/P7	Year 6/P7
16	12 books	6 books	Pack 3: 6 books	12 books	6 books	3 books			CD-ROM Pupils' Book Teacher's Guide	CD-ROM Pupil Book Teacher's Guide

P references relate to primary year groups in Northern Ireland

A closer look at the TreeTops components

TreeTops Fiction

TreeTops has a rich source of high quality fiction to engage and entertain children as they develop as readers. All the TreeTops books have been carefully levelled into eight stages that take children from developing fluency at Stage 9 to confident and skilled reading by Stage 16. In addition, as you can see from the charts on pages 85–89, the TreeTops fiction books have been levelled to the national curricula for England, Wales and Northern Ireland, and to Book Bands Levels.

A wide range of levelled *Fiction* titles cover all genres from humour to chillers. The TreeTops *Fiction* titles are written by well known authors including Geraldine McCaughrean, Martin Waddell and James Riordan, and contain vibrant illustrations. There is a *Teaching Notes* booklet to accompany each pack of six *Fiction* books, and notes inside the covers of each book give ideas for follow-up support which can be used either at school or at home.

- Well known author and illustrator – Sally Prue and Korky Paul
- Text and pictures designed to support readers who are just gaining fluency
- Humorous story and pictures make young readers want to read on

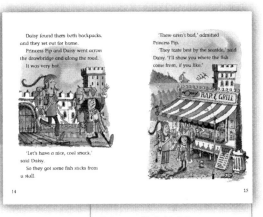

Princess Pip's Holiday
Stage 9 More Stories A *Fiction*

- Exciting historical story
- Links with cross-curricular work on the Second World War
- Text provides greater challenge for readers who are becoming more confident and experienced

Air Raid
Stage 14 More Stories A *Fiction*

- Helpful *Teaching Notes* for each pack of six books give ideas for reading, writing, speaking and listening and drama activities to support each book

TreeTops *Graphic Novels* are action-packed, take historical events as their inspiration and include non-fiction pages which give context to the stories. The thought-provoking themes of the *Graphic Novels* provide excellent stimulus for discussion, while the artwork and text totally engage readers.

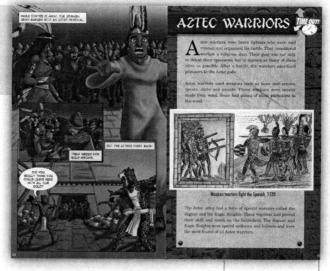

- Stunning illustrations integrated with motivating graphic novel style text
- Links to real historical events

- *Teaching Notes* with reading, writing, speaking and listening ideas to support each pack of six *Graphic Novels*

Cocoa Warriors
Stage 14
Graphic Novels

TreeTops *Classics* offer 24 classic titles that have been carefully adapted for juniors so that they can share the magic and mystery of these amazing stories. Children can confidently enjoy tales of suspense, excitement and adventure that would otherwise be out of their reach.

- Adaptations use language children can read and enjoy

- Adapted text written by well-established children's writers including Geraldine McCaughrean and Helena Pielichaty

The Secret Garden
Stage 14 *Classics*

- Detailed *Teaching Notes* to support each pack of six *Classics* – with cross-curricular links and suggestions of titles with similar themes

TreeTops *Playscripts* take some of the most popular TreeTops *Fiction* titles and present them in playscript form, with parts for five to eight children.

- Helps children develop reading fluency and speaking and listening skills
- Can be used in a fully dramatised performance or in a simple read-aloud session

Bertha's Secret Battle
Stage 11 *Playscripts*

TreeTops *Talking Stories* based on six popular TreeTops *Fiction* titles at Stages 10 and 11 allow children to work with the stories on screen, either individually or as a whole class. They can be used on the interactive whiteboard, and built-in tools allow you to highlight and annotate the text.

TreeTops *Myths and Legends* offer 24 books which contain a wide range of the oldest and most enduring stories in the world, retold by leading contemporary children's authors to bring out all of the action, drama, humour and depth of the original stories.

- Offer variety in style of writing and illustrations
- A letter from the author at the beginning of each book helps to introduce the book and allows children to consider the writers' craft

Tchang was about to run away, but the dragon called to him. 'Don't be frightened! I'm quite harmless. Tell me why you want to cross my river.'

Tchang explained that he needed to ask the Great Wizard of the West some important questions.

When the Pearl Dragon heard the questions, it smiled. 'You're a good lad, Tchang,' it said. 'Hop on my back and I'll have you across in a jiffy.'

On the far side of the river, Tchang thanked the dragon.

'Think nothing of it!' the dragon replied cheerfully. 'That's what I'm here for. Oh, by the way. While you're there, could you please ask the Wizard why I can't fly? Every dragon in China can fly – except me.'

Naturally, Tchang said yes. He set off again towards the West with the four questions going around and around in his head.

35

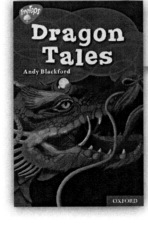

Dragon Tales
Stage 14 *Myths and Legends*

TreeTops Non-fiction

A wide range of levelled non-fiction titles cover all the non-fiction text types across Stages 9 to 16. Each non-fiction book has strong cross-curricular links (see the chart on pages 90–93 for a list of the main cross-curricular and subject-related links). The non-fiction books are perfect for guided or independent reading and for developing children's research skills. They can also be used as model texts, helping children to develop and structure their own non-fiction writing.

As for the fiction, a dedicated set of *Teaching Notes* for each pack of six books gives a range of ideas for literacy and cross-curricular activities with each book. The notes inside the covers give supportive guidance to parents or teaching assistants as they read the books with children.

- Topics that really interest and inspire children such as pirates, monsters, space and magicians
- Clear cross-curricular links
- Stunning photographs and clear page design to help children learn non-fiction reading skills

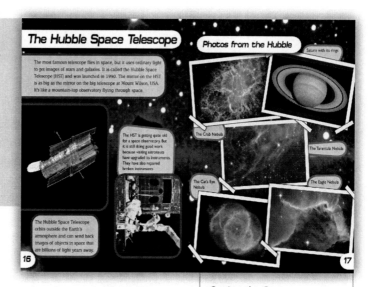

- *Teaching Notes* for each pack of six give suggestions for literacy and cross-curricular activities to support each book

Seeing the Stars
Stage 10 Pack *A* Non-Fiction

TreeTops *True Stories* provide a range of historical and contemporary biographies and narrative non-fiction that children will find engaging and fun to read. They make a good introduction to non-fiction for children who prefer narrative text, and also include a wide range of non-fiction features to support your non-fiction teaching.

- Fascinating true stories, such as the story of the discovery of Tutankhamun's tomb
- Narrative non-fiction style to hook readers in

Comprehension

TreeTops *Comprehension* gives you the resources you need for direct teaching of the full range of comprehension skills and strategies, as well as plenty of practice material for children to hone their developing comprehension skills. Interactive whiteboard activities and *Pupils' Books* provide lively and engaging activities based on TreeTops fiction and non-fiction, as well as poetry and high-quality children's trade books such as *Pippi Longstocking*, *The Highwayman* and *Tom's Midnight Garden*. All the core reading and comprehension skills are systematically addressed and explored through speaking and listening and drama, and direct engagement with the texts.

TreeTops *Group Activity Sheets* support and reinforce comprehension skills in the fiction books at Stages 9–16. As well as the photocopiable activity sheets, the book includes teacher guidance and personalised achievement records to track children's progress.

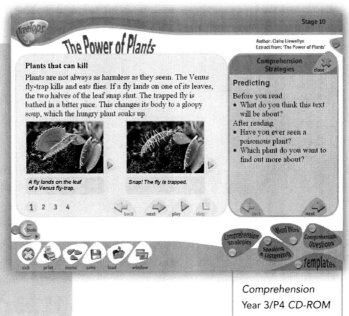

- The TreeTops *Comprehension CD-ROMs* are an ideal resource for whole-class teaching of the key comprehension strategies – questioning, predicting, clarifying, imagining and summarising
- The *Comprehension Pupils' Books* provide lots of practice and support for children as they learn to apply the comprehension strategies

Comprehension Year 3/P4 CD-ROM

- The *Comprehension Teacher's Guides* give step-by-step guidance on teaching comprehension and clear notes on using the *Comprehension CD-ROMs*

Writing

TreeTops *Storywriter*

With TreeTops *Storywriter* CD-ROMs you can plan and deliver successful whole-class writing lessons that lead children through the stages of writing a story.

The principles of Talk for Writing are embedded in the *Storywriter* methodology and you will find many opportunities for purposeful talk at each stage of the process. The *Pupil Books* which accompany the *CD-ROMs* allow children to take control of their own writing, with tips and ideas for more successful story writing.

Introducing the TreeTops authors

TreeTops includes fiction and non-fiction books by many of the finest authors writing for children today. Here are just some of the inspiring authors whose books are featured in TreeTops.

Geraldine McCaughrean is the award-winning author of over 140 books and plays. She writes everything from simple picture books to teen dramas and says she "tries never to write the same story twice". Geraldine was chosen, from a field of 200 authors around the world to write the sequel to J M Barrie's classic *Peter Pan* – *Peter Pan in Scarlet*, which has been described as "incredibly imaginative and quirky". You can find Geraldine McCaughrean's book **Noisy Neighbours** in TreeTops *Fiction*.

Martin Waddell writes all his books in the stone barn beside his home. He dreams his stories in his garden and on walks. He says that this is where he belongs. He has twice won the Smarties Award for his well loved stories *Farmer Duck* and *Can't You Sleep, Little Bear?* Martin also won the Hans Christian Andersen Award in 2004 for his contribution to children's literature. He loves a good ghost story because of the fun a ghost can add, as well as exploring how the past always affects the present. Martin has written a ghost story for TreeTops *Fiction* called **The Ghost Ship**, as well as **The Big Little Dinosaur** and **Cup Winners** for TreeTops *True Stories*.

Pippa Goodhart's favourite book ever is *Dogger* by Shirley Hughes. She writes books for children because they are a fresh audience, open to anything. She has been shortlisted for the Kathleen Fidler Award, the Smarties Prize and the Young Telegraph book of the Year and writes the hilarious new Winnie the Witch books under the pseudonym Laura Owen. Pippa has written a number of books for TreeTops including a retelling of the **The Jungle Book** by Rudyard Kipling for TreeTops *Classics*. Many of Pippa's stories for TreeTops are based on traditional tales such as **Sister Ella, Dick Whittington**, and **Tom Thumb and the Football Team**.

Pie Corbett has published over 250 books and several key educational schemes. He wrote the poetry objectives for the Literacy Framework and created the Talk for Writing materials and training. He works with the story museum and has written **Wolf Fables** for TreeTops *Myths and Legends* as well as being the series consultant for TreeTops *Storywriter*.

Paul Shipton wanted to be an astronaut, a footballer or a rock star when he was a child and is quite surprised to be an award-winning author. He says he wanted to write stories about animals which weren't cute or cuddly and so he wrote *Bug Muldoon and the Garden of Fear* followed by *The Pig Scrolls* and *The Pig Who Saved the World*, which won the Nestlé Children's Book Prize Bronze Award in 2006. Paul has written numerous titles for TreeTops *Fiction*, including **Pet Squad**, which follows his animal theme, **The Cowboy Next Door**, **The Ultimate Trainers**, **Billy's Luck** and **Half Price Hero**.

Paul Stewart has written over 50 books but is most famous for the fabulous *Edge Chronicles*, which he wrote in partnership with Chris Riddell. They enjoy working together so much that they live four doors away from each other in Brighton! Together they have also created the *Far-Flung Adventures* and *Barnaby Grimes*. Paul Stewart enjoys writing for children because children are such demanding readers – they won't tolerate boring bits! Paul has written **Snowblind** for TreeTops *Fiction*.

How TreeTops works for you

The TreeTops fiction, non-fiction, comprehension and writing resources are specially designed to help you teach literacy in an effective and enjoyable way, in line with the requirements of the modern curriculum.

TreeTops and the teaching of literacy

Recent thinking on the teaching of literacy has highlighted the two core areas word recognition or vocabulary development, and language comprehension. Both areas are dependent upon speaking and listening skills, and, as a result, speaking and listening has also been given a higher priority in language and literacy development.

In addition, the most effective language development takes place in the context of a broad and rich curriculum.

The wide range of TreeTops books has been developed for Key Stage 2 children with all these priorities in mind.

Word recognition and vocabulary development

By Key Stage 2, most children are developing fluency and independence in reading by using a range of techniques for decoding and acquiring new vocabulary. This vocabulary enrichment enhances language comprehension. The TreeTops books enable children to broaden and enrich this vocabulary, and *Teaching Notes* for each title give extra support to extend children's vocabulary development. TreeTops *Comprehension* also provides stimulating and enjoyable ways of extending children's vocabulary, both on screen and in the *Pupils' Books*.

The *Non-fiction* strand of TreeTops is particularly important for vocabulary development. Here children meet and understand technical and specialised words and concepts. Labelled pictures, diagrams and glossaries all enable the child to understand the meanings of new words and to read and learn independently.

Language comprehension

As children develop confidence and fluency in reading they become more sophisticated in their understanding of texts. In the suggested activities in the *Teaching Notes* for each Stage, in the TreeTops *Comprehension Pupils' Books* and in the TreeTops *Comprehension CD-ROMs* children will learn to:

- answer questions that require factual answers, deductions and inferences

- use their own experiences to connect with ideas and feelings

- make predictions

- summarise the main points of a paragraph, chapter or book

- make imaginative suggestions and comments.

Books from the wide range of genres available in TreeTops develop, stimulate and challenge the reading comprehension ability of children with a variety of interests and preferences.

Speaking and listening

The crucial role of competent speaking and listening skills has been emphasised in recent reports and recommendations.

- The TreeTops *Teaching Notes* for each pack provide suggested activities to enable children to discuss issues and ideas from the texts. The suggestions encourage children to work alone, in pairs and in small or large groups to enable role play, discussion, co-operation and the ability to engage with, and build upon, the ideas of others.

- The TreeTops *Comprehension CD-ROMs* offer many ideas and activities to encourage children to discuss and explore the featured texts together, using the full range of comprehension skills and strategies as they talk about what they are reading.

- The TreeTops *Comprehension Pupils' Books* include a range of stimulating partner activities for discussion, planning and role play, which allow children to develop their speaking and listening skills alongside their comprehension skills.

Shared, guided and independent reading

The TreeTops fiction and non-fiction books are ideal for use in independent, group, guided and shared reading right across Key Stage 2. Suggested activities for group, guided and independent reading are described in the *Teaching Notes* that accompany each TreeTops pack, and are linked to specific curricular objectives so that you can be sure children's reading skills are built up in a systematic and effective way.

The TreeTops *Comprehension CD-ROMs* may also be used for shared and guided reading with a focus on comprehension skills. Extracts from fiction, non-fiction and poetry texts appear on the screen with questions, suggestions and links to note-making grids and flow charts. The teacher can highlight aspects of the text, add notes and focus in on particular areas when working with a group or the whole class. Children can use the templates to create their own notes.

Writing

The books, both fiction and non-fiction, provide a wealth of stimulus material for writing in different genres, voices and formats. Ideas and support for writing activities based on each TreeTops book are available in the *Teaching Notes* that accompany each pack.

In addition, TreeTops *Storywriter* provides a specific focus on the direct teaching of writing. The software and *Pupil Books* for each year group guide the children through activities that will improve their creative writing, from planning to drafting, revising and publishing.

Meeting the needs of all your children

TreeTops provides a wide range of stories for use throughout Key Stage 2. In TreeTops *Fiction* each Stage allows plenty of choice for readers and plenty of practice at a comfortable level of challenge. This variety allows children to develop their own tastes and interests, and also to experiment with new genres, such as historical novels or science fiction, that may be new to them.

The TreeTops *Graphic Novels* provide a supportive context for children to develop confidence and competence in reading and in comprehension skills.

Some readers, often boys, prefer non-fiction to fiction. The varied format of non-fiction texts allows quick access to interesting material without the need to read an entire book. TreeTops *Non-fiction* provides a wide selection of beautifully illustrated books across a range of subject areas.

TreeTops *Classics* introduces texts that have entertained and delighted children and adults for many years. These abridged titles encourage able readers to turn to the original and give them the confidence to make more challenging choices of reading material. For less confident readers, the series offers an accessible introduction to classic stories from the past.

A rich and broad curriculum

A curriculum in which fluent oracy and literacy are fundamental to learning has always been at the heart of primary education. TreeTops *Fiction* and *Non-fiction* support a cross-curricular topic based approach to learning. Stories can be used to teach PHSE (e.g. *The Lie Detector*), History (e.g. *Climbing in the Dark*) and Science (e.g. *Waiting for Goldie*) to name just a few of the possible subject areas.

Non-fiction books directly support Science (e.g. *Animal Parents*), Mathematics (e.g. *What is Time?*), Art (e.g. *Amazing Paint!*), Geography (e.g. *Maps, Measurements and Meanings*), History (e.g. *Arms and Armour*), P.E. (*Sport is Fun!*), Literacy (e.g. *Let's Look at Adverts*) and Music (e.g. *Making Music*).

Further suggestions for cross-curricular links can be found on pages 97–101 of this *Teacher's Handbook*.

Assessment for Learning and personalisation

Assessment for Learning (AfL) is a way of involving children in the whole cycle of teaching and learning through:

- activating their prior knowledge

- sharing and making their own learning intentions

- understanding where they are on the way to reaching the learning intention

- having a clear set of success criteria so that they know what the outcome of their learning should look like

- identifying what they need to learn and do next.

AfL is central to using TreeTops as an effective literacy programme. The guidance for this and for involving your children in their learning are found in:

- clear curricular objectives for every book in the *Teaching Notes* accompanying every pack

- a checklist of reading skills for each Stage of TreeTops within pages 68–84 of this *Teacher's Handbook*

- self-assessment record sheets for each Stage of TreeTops found within pages 68–84 of this *Teacher's Handbook*

- suggestions for individual recommendations based on assessment in the 'Next steps' pages of this *Teacher's Handbook* (see pages 64–67).

TreeTops *Storywriter* and TreeTops *Comprehension* also include assessment guidance and support.

Case studies

Angela Pedley, Deputy Head Teacher and Literacy Co-ordinator at Ince Church of England Primary School, Higher Ince, Wigan

"Ince Church of England Primary School is a school with 350 pupils aged 3–11.

We use TreeTops *Fiction, Non-fiction, Classics, Graphic Novels* and *True Stories* for independent reading in Key Stage 2. We find that TreeTops provides us with the breadth that is needed in a reading programme. It allows the children to access books from a variety of genres and experience texts that other reading programmes perhaps wouldn't always provide them with the opportunity to. We encourage students to choose their own books for independent reading and find that with TreeTops levelling we can be confident that even when children are making their own selections they are reading books appropriate to the level they are reading at. The notes inside the covers are great for providing teaching assistants and parents with ideas to support the children's reading.

The variety of books in the TreeTops range means that all of our children are able to find a book that they enjoy reading; we have found that the non-fiction books have been particularly beneficial in raising boys' interest in reading throughout the school. We find that the illustrations, pictures, photographs and writing in the TreeTops books are extremely child-friendly, and we have absolutely no problem getting our children to read them. I have been walking the corridors on a number of occasions and heard children encouraging friends to read a particular book in the TreeTops range and even offering to show them where they can find it! It's great to find a junior reading programme with books that children really enjoy reading and will discuss without encouragement."

Andrew Edwards, Year 5 Class Teacher at Hangleton Junior School, Brighton & Hove

"Hangleton Junior School is a school with 368 pupils aged 7–11.

TreeTops *Comprehension* has really added to both my whole-class teaching and guided reading sessions. The children find the texts interesting and love the look of them on screen or on the SMART™ Board. The quality of the questioning included helps the children get to the heart of a text and allows me to easily spot gaps in their understanding. The related texts in the *Pupils' Book* follow on seamlessly and provide great opportunities for independent and group work. TreeTops *Comprehension* has injected a vibrancy to reading comprehension that was long overdue."

Karen Holmes, Head Teacher at St Tudy Church of England Primary School, Bodmin, Cornwall

"St Tudy Church of England Primary School is a village school with 65 pupils aged 4–11.

We are a very small school and therefore tend to buy a selection of TreeTops books rather than the larger packs. We use TreeTops *Fiction, Non-Fiction* and *Graphic Novels* within the school for both independent and guided reading. The children really enjoy reading the *Graphic Novels* and like the combination of both fiction and non-fiction that is contained within the books. We decided that before we purchased the *Graphic Novels* we would trial them with one of our students who has dyslexia and really didn't enjoy reading. He absolutely loved the books and went from just being able to read the Stage 10 and 11 *Fiction* and *Non-fiction* books to reading all of the Stage 13 *Graphic Novels* books. This collection of books really seemed to alter how he felt about reading and touched on subjects that he was interested in reading about.

Lower down in the school they use the *Teaching Notes* that accompany the TreeTops books in intervention sessions. The *Teaching Notes* provide teaching assistants with guidance to help further the children's reading skills and contain great ideas for getting more from the books and improving the children's comprehension."

Cheryl Whaley, Literacy Co-ordinator at Hempland Primary School, Heworth, York

"Hempland Primary School has 390 pupils on roll aged 4–11.

We primarily introduced TreeTops into the school to update our selection of home reading books. We chose TreeTops because it provides modern, durable books that are relevant to the children's interests. Parents have responded really positively to the books and have commented on how much the children enjoy reading them. Parents of boys have been particularly impressed with the interest that their children show in the books. We currently use TreeTops *Fiction, Non-fiction* and *Classics* books as home readers, but are hoping to invest in the *Graphic Novels* and use the books within guided reading sessions as well.

We also use TreeTops *Comprehension* within the school, using both the *Pupils' Books* and *CD-ROMs* during guided reading sessions. TreeTops *Comprehension* has proven to be an excellent resource and is often used by teaching assistants in intervention sessions."

TreeTops and the National Curricula

Wherever in the UK you are based, TreeTops can support you in your teaching of both literacy and the wider curriculum.

In England

TreeTops is fully in line with the Primary Framework for Literacy, and you can find detailed guidance and correlation to the Framework in the *Teaching Notes* for each TreeTops pack.

Speaking and listening

As well as providing a rich resource of motivating stories and non-fiction for children to read, TreeTops also supports the central role for **speaking and listening** in the curriculum.

- The *Teaching Notes* at each Stage give ideas for activities to support a wide range of speaking and listening skills, including oral rehearsal of ideas, working collaboratively, dialogic talk, drama and role play.

- TreeTops *Comprehension* explores quality texts and includes opportunities for paired and group work, discussion and role play.

- TreeTops *Storywriter* makes explicit the link between talk and writing in a way that children will find engaging and supportive as they develop as writers.

- TreeTops also includes a range of playscripts based on popular stories from the series, which can be used to help children empathise with the characters and make deeper connections with characters' motivations and actions. TreeTops *Playscripts* can be used for simple group reading activities or for a fully staged performance.

Understanding of language

- The TreeTops fiction and non-fiction texts use a rich variety of language, supported by glossaries where necessary to help children develop their vocabularies as they read.

- The texts are very carefully levelled to ensure that there is just enough challenge to motivate children. In this way children can tackle more complex ideas and themes such as those found in the TreeTops *Classics* series.

- TreeTops *Comprehension* breaks down key comprehension skills and shows children how to focus on the language, both at whole-text and sentence level.

ICT

- The *Teaching Notes* for each Stage include lots of ideas for using ICT in the context of exploring the TreeTops books.

- The TreeTops *Storywriter CD-ROMs* offer stimulating visual ideas for writing, interactive ways of planning writing and an interactive 'author assistant' to help children with their writing.

- TreeTops *Comprehension* offers software to help you explore texts together with the whole class, interact with the texts and teach comprehension skills interactively.

Reading

- TreeTops *Teaching Notes* offer plenty of support for using the books in guided, group and independent reading. The careful structure of TreeTops ensures that children's progression is well supported across a wide range of genres and reading levels. Home-school links in reading are also supported through the notes inside the cover of each book, which give parents ideas for discussing and sharing the books with their children.

- As well as supportive texts for children who are just beginning to become fluent readers, TreeTops also offers a range of more sophisticated reads. For example, TreeTops *Classics* offer children a route into some of the best-known and most enduring examples of classic literature, from *The Jungle Book* and *Black Beauty* to *Wuthering Heights* and *Macbeth*.

Writing and spelling

- The *Teaching Notes* for each Stage include ideas for writing that are inspired by the texts. They also include tips for exploring ideas from the texts further, as well as teaching key writing skills such as the use of connectives, sentence construction, sequencing, etc. Children's understanding of words is enhanced through the writing activities, and there are opportunities to support spelling across the curriculum, especially in the non-fiction texts.

- TreeTops *Comprehension* also offers a range of writing activities to support children's responses to texts.

- TreeTops *Storywriter* structures the writing process in a way that children will find motivating and enjoyable. It takes children through from planning their stories to drafting, editing and revising, and offers inspiring ideas for the final published outcome.

Links to the wider curriculum

History, Geography and PSHE

- There are *Non-fiction* books in TreeTops that support children's understanding of history, for example *Visual Vikings* at Stage 9, *War Children* at Stage 11 and *Celebrating Black History* at Stage 12. Historical themes also occur in some TreeTops *Fiction* stories, e.g. *Grace the Pirate* and *Air Raid!* at Stage 14, and *The Powder Monkey* at Stage 15. In addition, many of the TreeTops *Graphic Novels*, *Myths and Legends* and *True Stories* have a historical setting.

- Children's geographical understanding is supported by TreeTops *Non-fiction* books such as *Save Our Coasts* and *Under the Volcano* at Stage 13, and *Planet Granite* at Stage 16.

- Children's social understanding can be supported through books such as *Reach for the Skies* at Stage 15 and *Our Earth is Unique* at Stage 16 in the *Non-fiction* series, and the biographies of important figures such as Nelson Mandela in the *True Stories* series. Stories and playscripts such as *Stupid Trousers* at Stage 10 and *The Lie Detector* at Stage 12 can also be used to help children think about and discuss social issues.

Science and Technology

- Many of the TreeTops *Non-fiction* titles also support scientific and technological understanding, for example *Seeing the Stars* at Stage 10, *The Flick of a Switch* at Stage 12, *The Power of Nature* at Stage 14 and *Let's Go to the Planets* at Stage 16.

Maths

- Mathematical concepts come into several of the TreeTops *Non-fiction* books, including *What is Time?* at Stage 11 and *Maps, Measurements and Meanings* at Stage 14.

Physical development, health and wellbeing

- TreeTops *Non-fiction* books that can support children's learning in this area include *Against All Odds* at Stage 9, *Sport is Fun* at Stage 10, *A–Z of Survival* at Stage 11 and *Pests, Plagues and Parasites* at Stage 16.

The arts

- There are several TreeTops *Non-fiction* titles that will help children deepen their understanding of the arts, including *Picture This!* at Stage 9, *Amazing Paint*! at Stage 10 and *Making Music* at Stage 13.

  See pages 97 – 101 for more information about how TreeTops books can support a cross-curricular approach.

TreeTops and Assessing Pupils' Progress

- TreeTops contains a number of resources that will help you to gather evidence of children's progress for Assessing Pupils' Progess (APP) through the Assessment Focuses.

- Pages 36 – 63 in this *Teacher's Handbook* give detailed support for using a range of TreeTops books to assess children's reading and writing development in the context of APP.

- The curriculum coverage charts in the *Teaching Notes* for each pack show the main Assessment Focuses covered in each book, and also give a note of National Curriculum Levels.

- The questions and activities suggested in the *Teaching Notes* provide ample opportunity for teachers to gain evidence of children's attainment against the Assessment Focuses, and these can be used to contribute towards records kept for APP.

- The TreeTops *Comprehension Teacher's Guides* provide a comprehensive series of assessment grids which draw out the main Literacy Framework Objectives, learning intentions, success criteria and Assessment Focuses for each unit. This will help to keep track of formative assessment and contribute to the picture of children's holistic development which is built up as part of APP. In addition, the units in the TreeTops *Comprehension Pupils' Books* all have an Assessment Focus and are differentiated to support children at different National Curriculum Levels within the year group.

- Guidance on National Curriculum Levels is contained in the TreeTops Fiction and Non-fiction overview charts on pages 85 – 93.

In Wales

TreeTops will help you address every aspect of English in the National Curriculum for Wales at Key Stage 2. It offers excellent scope for encouraging children to read widely, for both enjoyment and information, in the context of progressively more challenging and demanding texts. It also offers activities and support for developing children's communication/speaking and listening skills, and an excellent range of examples of different text types that will act as models for children's writing.

The Curriculum coverage charts in the *Teaching Notes* for each TreeTops pack show how each TreeTops book relates to English in the National Curriculum for Wales, and the charts on pages 85–93 of this *Teacher's Handbook* also offer an overview of the relevant National Curriculum for Wales Levels. The notes below show how TreeTops supports each of the key areas in the curriculum for English at Key Stage 2.

Oracy

The *Teaching Notes* for each TreeTops pack include a range of speaking and listening activities developed to support each TreeTops title. The activities help children to develop their skills in:

• exploring, developing and explaining ideas

• sharing ideas, insights and opinions

• reading aloud, telling and enacting stories

• reporting and describing events and observations

• presenting and performing, live or on tape.

As the TreeTops books develop in complexity throughout Key Stage 2, the opportunities for oracy activities become more complex and demanding to match children's developing skills.

TreeTops *Comprehension* and TreeTops *Storywriter* also offer rich opportunities for developing children's oracy in the context of purposeful comprehension and writing activities.

Reading

The wide range of stories and non-fiction texts in TreeTops encompass all of the main text types children are expected to meet at Key Stage 2. As the programme is carefully structured, the texts increase in complexity gradually from Stage to Stage, allowing children plenty of practice as they develop as enthusiastic, independent and reflective readers.

The TreeTops *Teaching Notes* and *Comprehension* resources offer lots of ideas for helping children to understand and respond imaginatively to the texts they read. TreeTops *Comprehension* explicitly teaches the skills of inference, deduction and prediction which children need to develop as they progress as readers within the context of both fiction and non-fiction.

Writing

The TreeTops fiction and non-fiction books can be used as models for children's writing across the full range of text types, and the *Teaching Notes* for each pack give a range of rich ideas for writing activities to help children follow up and respond to each story or non-fiction text. There are opportunities to focus on writing skills such as planning, drafting, revising and evaluating written work. The writing ideas also offer scope for focusing on children's punctuation, spelling and handwriting in the context of motivating writing activities linked to their reading.

In addition, TreeTops *Storywriter* offers children a clear model for planning, writing, developing and publishing their own stories based on a reading of model texts. All of the TreeTops resources allow children to develop their writing skills gradually and systematically as they progress through Key Stage 2.

Guidance on National Curriculum for Wales Levels is contained in the TreeTops Fiction and Non-fiction overview charts on pages 85–93.

In Northern Ireland

TreeTops is fully in line with the requirements of the revised Northern Ireland Curriculum for Language and Literacy. It provides many opportunities to cover the objectives for talking and listening, reading, and writing at the end of Key Stage 1 and throughout Key Stage 2.

The Curriculum coverage charts in the *Teaching Notes* for each TreeTops pack show how each TreeTops book relates to the Northern Ireland Curriculum for Language and Literacy, and the charts on pages 85–93 of this *Teacher's Handbook* also offer an overview of the relevant Northern Ireland Curriculum Levels. The notes below show how TreeTops supports each of the key areas in the curriculum for Language and Literacy at the end of Key Stage 1 and throughout Key Stage 2.

Talking and listening

Built into the TreeTops *Teaching Notes* for each pack are a range of activities and ideas for talking and listening, relevant to each individual TreeTops book. This means that while children are reading as a group, or after they have finished reading a specific book, they have opportunities to discuss and share ideas about their reading. This not only enriches the reading experience, but it also helps them to learn how to communicate effectively in groups, taking turns, encouraging others to join in, giving reasons for their views and justifying their opinions.

Drama and improvisation ideas are included for many of the books, and all of the TreeTops texts offer opportunities for children to practise reading aloud with appropriate inflection and expression.

Opportunities for purposeful talking and listening are also built into TreeTops *Comprehension* (both through the *CD-ROMs* and *Pupils' Books*) and TreeTops *Storywriter*.

Reading

The importance of a wide range of different texts and reading activities, both on paper and in electronic formats, is stressed in the Curriculum for Language and Literacy. TreeTops offers stories and non-fiction texts across the full range of text types recommended for children at the end of Key Stage 1 and throughout Key Stage 2. It also offers, in the form of the *Talking Stories*, TreeTops *Comprehension* and TreeTops *Storywriter*, a range of motivating and inspiring multimedia texts for children to explore on screen.

The TreeTops texts are carefully levelled, ensuring that children's reading skills develop systematically as they increase their reading stamina to tackle longer and more complex books. The *Teaching Notes* for each pack offer detailed activities for use in group and individual reading, to ensure that children think about and explore the texts appropriately as they read. The notes inside the covers of each book offer guidance for teachers, parents and other adults who may be reading with the children, to help them get the most from their reading.

TreeTops *Comprehension* offers a systematic way to develop children's reading and comprehension skills at the end of Key Stage 1 and throughout Key Stage 2.

Writing

The curriculum stresses the importance of writing for a variety of audiences and in a range of contexts, using both traditional and electronic formats. The *Teaching Notes* for each TreeTops pack offer a wide range of engaging writing activities that encourage children to reflect on and respond to their reading, whilst developing their writing skills. The writing activities vary from short tasks that can be accomplished in a half-hour session to longer activities that may take several sessions to complete. The TreeTops books themselves offer strong models for children's writing, across both fiction and non-fiction text types.

TreeTops *Storywriter* offers children detailed guidance on drafting, revising, improving, publishing and evaluating their own stories, breaking down what can seem like a complex task into achievable stages. This develops children's confidence as writers and allows them to progress from simple writing tasks to more complex ones as they work through the programme at the end of Key Stage 1 and throughout Key Stage 2.

Guidance on Northern Ireland Curriculum Levels is contained in the TreeTops Fiction and Non-fiction overview charts on pages 85–93.

How the TreeTops resources work together

The diagrams on the following pages show how the TreeTops resources at each Stage fit together to help you teach reading, writing, speaking and listening in a seamless way. A sample book has been selected from each Stage, and a topic web shows the main TreeTops resources that link to and support this book, demonstrating the range of resources available in TreeTops and the depth of curriculum coverage.

The bullet points below each topic web show the main ways in which the featured resources can be used.

The selected books are just examples to show you how TreeTops works – similar linked resources are available for most TreeTops titles at each Stage.

Stage 9 example book: *Captain Comet and the Dog Star*

Linked resources

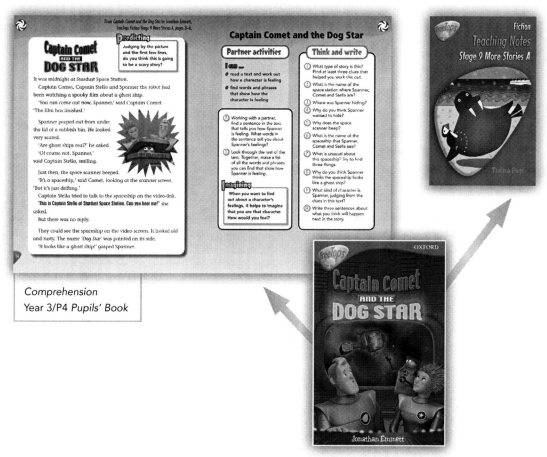

Comprehension
Year 3/P4 *Pupils' Book*

Using the linked resources

Stage 9 *Fiction* More Stories A *Captain Comet and the Dog Star*

- Ideal for group, guided or independent reading.
- Use the notes inside the cover for quick and simple activity ideas to support children as they read.
- The notes can be used for classroom activities or for homework ideas.

Stage 9 *Fiction* More Stories A *Teaching Notes*

Contains a wealth of ideas for using *Captain Comet and the Dog Star* with a group, including:

- tips to help you introduce the story
- ideas to focus on characterisation and the build-up of characters' emotions
- activities to use during the reading process
- ideas for speaking and listening activities linked to the book
- tips to help the children respond to the story and use inference
- follow-up writing activities.

Comprehension Year 3/P4: *Pupils' Book*

- The *Pupils' Book* contains an extract from *Captain Comet and the Dog Star* and comprehension activities to help groups, pairs and individuals practise a range of comprehension strategies, including predicting and imagining.

Stage 10 example book: *Stupid Trousers*

Linked resources

Comprehension
Year 3/P4 *CD-ROM*

Comprehension
Year 3/P4 *Pupils' Book*

Stages 10–11
Talking Stories *CD-ROM*

Comprehension
Year 3/P4
Teacher's Guide

Using the linked resources

Stage 10 *Fiction* More Stories A *Stupid Trousers*

- Ideal for group, guided or independent reading.
- Use the notes inside the cover for ideas to support the children as they read.
- The notes can be used for classroom activities or for homework ideas.

Stage 10 *Fiction* More Stories A *Teaching Notes*

Contains plenty of purposeful ideas for using *Stupid Trousers* with a group, including:

- a synopsis and tips to help you introduce the story
- ideas to focus on characterisation and the theme of the story
- activities to explore the characters' emotions and motivation
- ideas to explore the story through role play
- tips to help the children respond to the story and use inference
- follow-up writing activities.

Comprehension Year 3/P4: CD-ROM, Pupils' Book and Teacher's Guide

- Use the *CD-ROM* to read an extract from *Stupid Trousers* adapted as a playscript. Compare it with the narrative form. Use the *Teacher's Guide* suggestions and on-screen comprehension activities to develop children's confidence in making deductions and inferences.

- Use the *Stupid Trousers* playscript extract in the *Pupils' Book* to act out part of the story. Children can work in pairs or independently to answer the 'Think and write' questions.

Stage 10 – Stage 11 *Talking Stories CD-ROM*

- Use the talking story to discuss the events and characters. Picture hotspots show what characters are thinking. Answer predictive questions.

- Use the highlighter tool to highlight the text for word and sentence work.

- Use the questions at the end for children to answer orally or in writing.

Stage 10 *Playscripts Stupid Trousers*

- Read the playscript after reading the story. Compare the two ways of telling a story.

- Ideal to develop group play-reading and presentation.

- Teaches awareness of the importance of stage directions and the implications for reading with expression.

Stage 11 example book: *War Children*

Linked resources

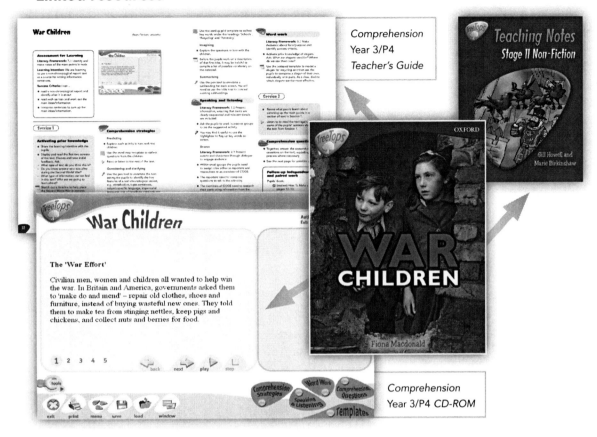

Using the linked resources

Stage 11 *Non-fiction War Children*

- Ideal for group, guided or independent reading.
- Use the notes inside the cover for ideas to support the children as they read, and for homework ideas.

Stage 11 *Non-fiction Teaching Notes*

The notes provide a variety of focused activities to develop children's reading skills, including:

- tips to help you discuss the features of non-fiction books
- ideas to develop children's vocabulary
- activities to help children absorb new information and relate it to what they already know
- ideas for speaking and listening activities linked to the subject matter
- tips to help children find and record information
- follow-up writing activities.

Comprehension Year 3/P4: *CD-ROM* and *Teacher's Guide*

- Read an extract from *War Children* on the *CD-ROM* together. Encourage children to use the highlighter tool to select important words. Show them how to use the notepad to note important words and information they want to remember.
- Use further suggestions in the *Comprehension Teacher's Guide* to practise a range of comprehension strategies, note taking and role play ideas.

Stage 12 example book: *The Lie Detector* (Playscript)

Linked resources

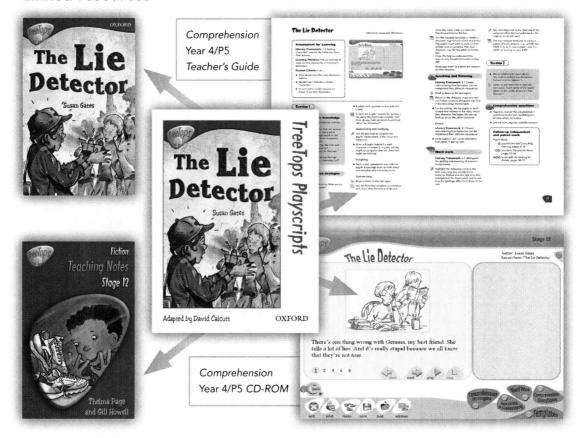

Using the linked resources

Stage 12 *Playscripts The Lie Detector*

- Ideal to develop group play-reading and presentation.
- Teaches awareness of the importance of stage directions and the implications for reading with expression.

Stage 12 *Fiction The Lie Detector*

- Read the story together or independently. Compare the story and the playscript, e.g. descriptions of characters, settings and events.
- Discuss which genre has more impact on the reader.

Stage 12 *Fiction Teaching Notes*

The notes contain ideas for using the story with the class:

- tips to help you introduce the story also apply to the playscript
- use ideas for returning and responding to the text, bearing in mind that the narrator in the story is Laura in the play
- ideas for speaking and listening activities also apply to the play.

Comprehension Year 4/P5: *CD-ROM* and *Teacher's Guide*

- Use the *CD-ROM* to listen to the play. Discuss what was fair and unfair.
- Use ideas in the *Teacher's Guide* to teach children to record their ideas in various formats: annotations, speech bubbles, character maps, mind maps.
- Use the comprehension questions to develop children's ability to make inferences and deductions from characters' actions.

Stage 13 example book: *The Golden Scarab*

Linked resources

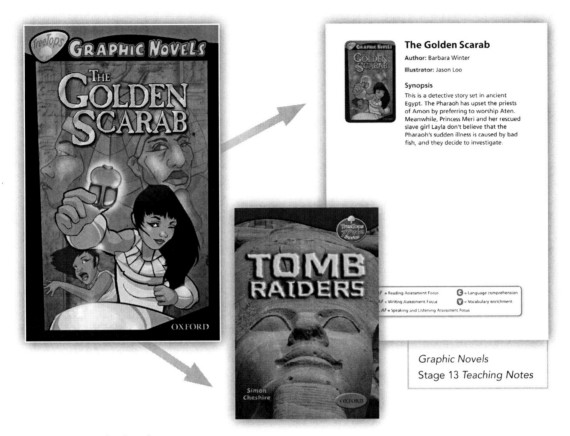

Using the linked resources

Stage 13 *Graphic Novels The Golden Scarab*

- Use this exciting picture story to stimulate interest and motivate all readers, especially boys.
- Ideal for introducing cross-curricular work on Ancient Egypt.
- Teaches storytelling through dialogue and succinct sentences.
- Non-fiction pages between chapters supply factual background information.
- The notes inside the cover can be used for classroom activities or for homework ideas.

Stage 13 *Graphic Novels Teaching Notes*

Contain a wealth of ideas for using *The Golden Scarab* story with a group. The notes provide:

- tips for getting the best out of this format in 'Introducing the book'
- questions to encourage deductions and inferences from both text and illustrations
- suggestions to support discussion to differentiate between fact and fiction
- speaking and listening suggestions encouraging children to reflect on the story
- ideas for writing activities which help children to reflect on their writing.

TreeTops *True Stories* Stages 13–14 *Tomb Raiders*

- This is the story of Howard Carter's discovery of Tutankhamun's tomb told from the point of view of a water boy who discovered the entrance to the tomb.
- Compare different versions of events and discuss the difference between fiction and non-fiction.

Stage 14 example book: *The Secret Garden*

Linked resources

Using the linked resources

Stage 14 *Classics The Secret Garden*

- This retelling of Frances Hodgson Burnett's classic story is ideal for group, guided or independent reading.

- Use the notes inside the cover for talking points and oral comprehension.

- Asterisks in the text denote words that are explained on pages 78–80. Use these to develop children's vocabulary and understanding of the context.

- Read the notes about the author and the adapter on pages 76–77. Discover what inspired Frances Hodgson Burnett and why Helena Pielichaty thinks it is a timeless story.

Stage 14 *Classics Teaching Notes*

The notes provide reading, writing, and speaking and listening ideas for using *The Secret Garden* with a group or class. They include:

- questions to encourage children to make deductions and inferences, using evidence from the text

- ideas for developing children's imagination

- writing activities that encourage children to make bold vocabulary choices.

Comprehension Year 5/P6: CD-ROM

- Choose *Tom's Midnight Garden* (*Oxford Children's Modern Classics*) on the CD-ROM to read from the screen or whiteboard. Compare the two children and the two gardens.

- Use the highlighter tool to locate and discuss unfamiliar words and phrases. Ask children to put these into their own words.

- Use the notepad to record similarities and differences between this story and *The Secret Garden*.

Stage 15 example book: *Pirates*

Linked resources

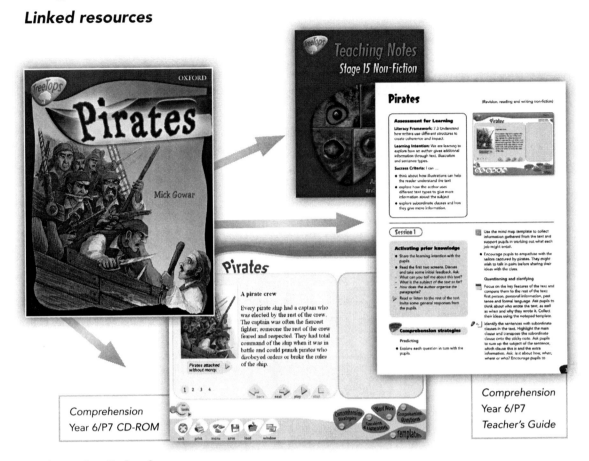

Comprehension
Year 6/P7 CD-ROM

Comprehension
Year 6/P7
Teacher's Guide

Using the linked resources

Stage 15 *Non-fiction Pirates*

This book includes photographs of source materials, an index, a glossary, text boxes and captions, making it ideal for teaching the features of non-fiction texts.

- Use the notes inside the cover for talking points and comprehension. These notes are also useful for reading at home and homework ideas.
- Use the quiz on page 30 of the book to discuss the concept of piracy in our world.

Stage 15 *Non-fiction Teaching Notes*

The notes contain a wealth of ideas for using *Pirates* with a group or class. They include:

- tips for introducing the book and noticing non-fiction features
- suggestions for managing new vocabulary
- ideas for interacting with the text in paired and group activities
- suggestions for creative writing based on the text.

Comprehension Year 6/P7: *CD-ROM* and *Teacher's Guide*

- Use the extract from *Pirates* to consider the way sentence structure varies to provide additional information.
- Answer the *CD-ROM* comprehension questions orally or in writing. (Check the answers in the *Teacher's Guide*).
- Use the highlighter tool to focus on sentence construction and vocabulary.
- Use the notepad to teach effective methods of note making.

Stage 16 example book: *Tales of the Underworld*

Linked resources

Comprehension
Year 6/P7 Pupils' Book

Using the linked resources

Stage 16 *Myths and Legends Tales of the Underworld*

This book retells four myths from different cultures that consider the world, life and death.

- Use the notes inside the cover for talking points and comprehension. These notes are also useful for reading at home and homework ideas.
- Use the author's letter to the reader on page 2 to introduce the book.

Stage 16 *Myths and Legends Teaching Notes*

The notes contain a wealth of ideas for using *Tales of the Underworld* with a group or class. They include:

- background information to help with introducing the book
- suggestions for managing new vocabulary
- ideas for interacting with the text in paired and group activities
- suggestions for creative writing based on the text.

Comprehension Year 6/P7: Pupils' Book

- You could use the extract from *Greek Battles* to make cross-curricular links with the Greek myth of Orpheus and Eurydice.

Assessment and planning

In this section, you will find a variety of resources to help you assess children's reading and writing skills using TreeTops resources. You will also find a wealth of handy information to help you plan your teaching.

The Assessment and planning section contains the following resources:

Assessing reading and writing with Treetops

The charts on pages 36–63 give focused assessment prompts and ideas to help you use specific books from TreeTops Stages 9 to 16 as part of your Assessment for Learning at Levels 2 to 5 of the National Curriculum in England. They can be used to collect evidence for APP (Assessing Pupils' Progress). For each TreeTops Stage we have picked an exemplar book to assess a wide range of skills across the areas of reading and writing, linked to the Assessment Focuses. Detailed questions and assessment tasks are provided for each book, linked to a specific National Curriculum Level. Where the same book can be used to assess more than one level, we have provided assessment prompts and ideas for both relevant levels so that you can pick the one most appropriate for your children. Before beginning the reading and writing assessments with the children, set aside time for them to read and think about the book. It will also be helpful to have a 'book talk' conversation about the book before using the suggested assessment prompts. You can use open questions ("Tell me what you think about …", "Why do you think he …?", "What makes you think that?" etc.) to encourage children to talk freely about the book and develop their own ideas.

Next steps

The charts on pages 64–67 provide ideas to help develop specific reading skills you have identified in the assessment process.

Skills checklists

Pages 68–84 present checklists of the reading skills children are likely to be developing at each Stage of TreeTops. You can use these checklists as a quick assessment tool, or for record keeping. As well as a teacher's version, there is a child's version of each checklist (self-assessment sheet), with the skills expressed clearly in terms of 'I can …' statements. These can be used for children's self-assessment.

TreeTops Fiction and Non-fiction overview charts and Curriculum Levels

The charts on pages 85–93 gather together a lot of useful information on the TreeTops books in one place. They show the Curriculum Levels in England, Wales and Northern Ireland for each Stage. They also indicate the Book Band Levels and provide age guidance. The charts provide information on the genres covered at each Stage and the main cross-curricular links.

TreeTops and the wider curriculum

On pages 97–101, you will find a cross-curricular topic web for each TreeTops Stage to show you how books from that Stage will fit into key cross-curricular topics.

Assessing reading and writing with TreeTops

Assessment Pointers for Stage 9/National Curriculum Level 2 (based on Stage 9 *Fiction More Stories A Captain Comet and the Dog Star*)

Reading assessment

Use the chart below to help you gather information to assess children's attainment against the Reading Assessment Focuses at Level 2.

Level 2 Assessment Focus guidelines	Suggested prompt	Notes on child's response	Ideas for following up child's response	Best fit NC Level
AF1 Range of key words read on sight; Unfamiliar words decoded using appropriate strategies (e.g. blending sounds); Some fluency and expression	When the child has finished reading the book, ask them to choose a page that they think is particularly exciting and read it aloud to you.		Does the child attempt a fluent pace in their reading? Do they sound out unfamiliar words? Do they recognise key high-frequency words on sight?	☐ L2 not attained ☐ Low 2 ☐ Secure 2 ☐ High 2
AF2 Some specific, straightforward information recalled; Generally a clear idea of where to look for information	Ask: *What did the Dog Star look like? Can you find some sentences that describe it?*		Notice whether the child can find the right place in the book easily and can find a description of the Dog Star.	☐ L2 not attained ☐ Low 2 ☐ Secure 2 ☐ High 2
AF3 Simple, plausible inference about events and information, using evidence from text	Ask: *What kind of character is Spanner? What is he like? How do you know?*		Does the child show some basic understanding of Spanner's character? Can they identify some parts of the text that show this (e.g. his speech)?	☐ L2 not attained ☐ Low 2 ☐ Secure 2 ☐ High 2
AF4 Some awareness of use of features of organisation, e.g. beginning and ending of story	Ask: *Can you find the start of the story? How do you know that is the start? What is happening at the start of the story?*		Check the child can confidently locate the start of the story. Encourage them to skim read the first few pages to remind them what happens at the start of the story.	☐ L2 not attained ☐ Low 2 ☐ Secure 2 ☐ High 2
AF5 Some effective language choices noted	Say: *Look at pages 14 and 15. Can you find a good word or phrase the writer uses to tell us what kind of character Nova is?*		The obvious phrase is 'evil smile' on page 15. Does the child spot this? Can they give a reason for their choice of word?	☐ L2 not attained ☐ Low 2 ☐ Secure 2 ☐ High 2
AF6 Simple statements about likes and dislikes in reading, sometimes with reasons	Ask: *Do you think this is an exciting story? Why or why not?*		Can the child give some reasons why they found the story exciting (or not)?	☐ L2 not attained ☐ Low 2 ☐ Secure 2 ☐ High 2
AF7 Some awareness that books are set in different times and places	Ask: *Where is the story set? Does the story take place nowadays, or in the future? How do you know?*		If the child has difficulty judging the setting and time frame of the story, give them some contemporary stories from Stage 9 with a realistic setting to look at (e.g. *Noisy Neighbours*). What are the differences between these story settings?	☐ L2 not attained ☐ Low 2 ☐ Secure 2 ☐ High 2

© Oxford University Press: 2010 Copying permitted within purchasing school only

Writing assessment

Ask the child to write a short adventure story about the crew of a spaceship. Suggest that the spaceship lands on a strange planet, or meets another spaceship. What might happen? How will their heroes overcome dangers? How will the story end?

Use the chart below to help you gather information from this piece of writing to assess children's attainment against the Writing Assessment Focuses at Level 2.

Level 2 Assessment Focus guidelines	Notes on child's writing	Ideas for following up child's writing	Best fit NC Level
AF1 Mostly relevant ideas and content, sometimes repetitive or sparse; Some apt word choices create interest		Is the content appropriate for a space story? Are there some attempts to use interesting and appropriate vocabulary?	☐ L2 not attained ☐ Low 2 ☐ Secure 2 ☐ High 2
AF2 Some basic purpose established; Some appropriate features of the form used		Does the child use a style that's broadly appropriate to a space story? Do they stick to their storyline or wander off on a different track?	☐ L2 not attained ☐ Low 2 ☐ Secure 2 ☐ High 2
AF3 Some basic sequencing of ideas or material; Openings and/or closings sometimes signalled		Does the child organise the story so that the reader can understand it, e.g. by sticking to chronological order? Does their story have a clear beginning and ending?	☐ L2 not attained ☐ Low 2 ☐ Secure 2 ☐ High 2
AF4 Ideas in sections grouped by content; some linking by simple pronouns		Does the child use paragraphs, or group related ideas together within the story? Do they use some pronouns to link sentences?	☐ L2 not attained ☐ Low 2 ☐ Secure 2 ☐ High 2
AF5 Some variation in sentence openings; Mainly simple sentences with 'and' used to connect clauses; Past and present tense generally consistent		Does the child use some different sentence openings, e.g. not always opening with the name of a character? Do they use 'and' correctly to connect clauses? Is their use of tense consistent?	☐ L2 not attained ☐ Low 2 ☐ Secure 2 ☐ High 2
AF6 Clause structure mostly grammatically correct; Sentence demarcation with capital letters and full stops usually accurate; Some accurate use of question and exclamation marks, and commas in lists		Does the child use capital letters and full stops correctly? Do most of their sentences make grammatical sense?	☐ L2 not attained ☐ Low 2 ☐ Secure 2 ☐ High 2
AF7 Simple, often speech-like vocabulary conveys relevant meanings; Some adventurous word choices		Does the child use vocabulary in a way that shows they know the meaning of the words? Do they sometimes use interesting words, e.g. words picked up from their reading?	☐ L2 not attained ☐ Low 2 ☐ Secure 2 ☐ High 2
AF8 Usually correct spelling of high frequency grammatical function words; common single-morpheme words; likely errors with inflected endings or phonetic attempts at vowel digraphs		Does the child make phonetically plausible attempts to spell words with vowel digraphs? Look at any spelling mistakes to assess patterns of error. Are there spelling patterns that need practice?	☐ L2 not attained ☐ Low 2 ☐ Secure 2 ☐ High 2

© Oxford University Press: 2010

Copying permitted within purchasing school only

Assessment Pointers for Stage 10/National Curriculum Level 2 (based on Stage 10 Fiction More Stories A *Stupid Trousers*)

Reading assessment

Use the chart below to help you gather information to assess children's attainment against the Reading Assessment Focuses at Level 2.

Level 2 Assessment Focus guidelines	Suggested prompt	Notes on child's response	Ideas for following up child's response	Best fit NC Level
AF1 Some fluency and expression, taking account of punctuation	Ask the child to read Chapter 1 aloud.		Did they notice speech marks and exclamation marks and read accordingly? Did they notice words such as 'shouted' and 'yelled' and respond with expression in their reading?	☐ L2 not attained ☐ Low 2 ☐ Secure 2 ☐ High 2
AF2 Some specific, straightforward information recalled	Ask the child to explain the title. Ask them to say why Ross did not want to wear the trousers.		Has the child understood the main points of the story? Can they explain the problem in general terms without rereading the story?	☐ L2 not attained ☐ Low 2 ☐ Secure 2 ☐ High 2
AF3 Comments based on textual cues, sometimes misunderstood	Ask the child to explain how many times the trousers were shortened, and who did it. Ask: *Why did Ross thank his brother at the end?*		Notice whether the child has realised that three people tried to shorten the trousers, making them too short to wear. Have they understood that Lee saved Ross from wearing the trousers?	☐ L2 not attained ☐ Low 2 ☐ Secure 2 ☐ High 2
AF4 Some awareness of use of features of organisation	Ask the child whether this book has chapters. Find pages where a new chapter begins.		Talk about what happens in each chapter. Notice whether the child contributes their own ideas.	☐ L2 not attained ☐ Low 2 ☐ Secure 2 ☐ High 2
AF5 Some effective language choices noted	Ask the child whether they have noticed any powerful verbs in the story. Ask them to scan the text to find more.		Does the child recognise that the author uses several words instead of 'said' and instead of 'went'. Can they explain why they are effective?	☐ L2 not attained ☐ Low 2 ☐ Secure 2 ☐ High 2
AF6 Simple statements about likes and dislikes in reading, sometimes with reasons	After reading, ask the child to tell you which part of the story they liked best. Ask them to say whether they like stories or information books best.		Can the child express a preference? Can they give a reason?	☐ L2 not attained ☐ Low 2 ☐ Secure 2 ☐ High 2
AF7 Some awareness that books are set in different times and places	Discuss the setting for this book. Ask: *What do we know about the place where they live? Is it set nowadays, or in the past?* Look at pictures in a historical story such as *A Kitten in Daisy Street* (TreeTops *Fiction* More Stories B Stage 12) and make comparisons.		Does the child take clues from the story and the illustrations to identify the setting? Do they recognise that *A Kitten in Daisy Street* is set at a different time? Can they make comparisons about the locations?	☐ L2 not attained ☐ Low 2 ☐ Secure 2 ☐ High 2

© Oxford University Press: 2010

Copying permitted within purchasing school only

Writing assessment

Ask the child to retell the story of *Stupid Trousers* using the title 'Pageboy Trousers' or similar. Discuss what happens in each chapter in the book and agree on four chapter headings. Ask the child to write the story in their own words, using the chapter headings.

Use the chart below to help you gather information from this piece of writing to assess children's attainment against the Writing Assessment Focuses at Level 2.

Level 2 Assessment Focus guidelines	Notes on child's writing	Ideas for following up child's writing	Best fit NC Level
AF1 Some apt word choices create interest		Has the child used words other than those in the story? Are they well chosen to describe characters or events?	☐ L2 not attained ☐ Low 2 ☐ Secure 2 ☐ High 2
AF2 Some attempts to adopt appropriate style		Has the child kept the author's lively style with lots of direct speech? Have they told the story in a way that holds the reader's interest?	☐ L2 not attained ☐ Low 2 ☐ Secure 2 ☐ High 2
AF3 Some basic sequencing of ideas, e.g. time-related words or phrases		Has the child used the chapter headings to create a logical sequence of events? Are there some time-related phrases ('later that night', 'next day', etc.)?	☐ L2 not attained ☐ Low 2 ☐ Secure 2 ☐ High 2
AF4 Ideas in sections grouped by content, some linking by simple pronouns		Does the writing focus on describing the sequence of events? Is the story easy to follow? Are pronouns used to avoid repetition of names?	☐ L2 not attained ☐ Low 2 ☐ Secure 2 ☐ High 2
AF5 Some variation in sentence openings; Past and present tense generally consistent		Does the child begin sentences with a variety of words other than names or pronouns? Is the story told consistently in the past tense? Is the present tense used in direct speech appropriately and consistently?	☐ L2 not attained ☐ Low 2 ☐ Secure 2 ☐ High 2
AF6 Sentence demarcation with capital letters and full stops usually accurate; Some accurate use of question and exclamation marks, and commas in lists		Does the child use capital letters and full stops correctly in sentences? Are question marks and exclamation marks used consistently? Are commas used correctly in lists?	☐ L2 not attained ☐ Low 2 ☐ Secure 2 ☐ High 2
AF7 Simple, often speech-like vocabulary conveys relevant meanings		Is the vocabulary used in direct speech relevant and appropriate? Is the storytelling vocabulary appropriate?	☐ L2 not attained ☐ Low 2 ☐ Secure 2 ☐ High 2
AF8 Usually correct spelling of high frequency grammatical function words		Are high frequency words spelled correctly?	☐ L2 not attained ☐ Low 2 ☐ Secure 2 ☐ High 2

Assessment Pointers for Stage 11/National Curriculum Level 2 (based on Stage 11 Non-fiction War Children)

Reading assessment

Use the chart below to help you gather information to assess children's attainment against the Reading Assessment Focuses at Level 2.

Level 2 Assessment Focus guidelines	Suggested prompt	Notes on child's response	Ideas for following up child's response	Best fit NC Level
AF1 Unfamiliar words decoded using appropriate strategies, e.g. blending sounds	Ask the child to read the contents list. Note their strategies for reading new words. As there are no pictures or context they will need to rely on phonic knowledge.		Note the child's strategies and whether they are able to segment and blend words effectively. Can they recognise spelling patterns such as 'au' and 'ion'? Were there any words that the child could not read independently?	☐ L2 not attained ☐ Low 2 ☐ Secure 2 ☐ High 2
AF2 Generally clear idea of where to look for information	Ask the child to show you a page where you can find out about children in the war.		Notice the strategies used: looking at the contents and index, and scanning headings. Did they find appropriate information?	☐ L2 not attained ☐ Low 2 ☐ Secure 2 ☐ High 2
AF3 Simple, plausible inference about events and information, using evidence from text; Comments based on textual cues, sometimes misunderstood	Read pages 8 and 9 together. Ask the child to tell you what it was like to be evacuated. Read page 7 together. Discuss why air-raid shelters were necessary.		Has the child realised that evacuation was not unpleasant for everyone? Can they make a sensible statement about it? Has the child understood why air-raid shelters were necessary? Can they explain how they were built?	☐ L2 not attained ☐ Low 2 ☐ Secure 2 ☐ High 2
AF4 Some awareness of use of features of organisation	Ask the child where they would find the Introduction in this book. Ask them to say what the pages headed 'Divided families' might be about. Ask them to find the right page.		Did the child know that the Introduction is at the beginning? Did they suggest using the Contents and Index pages to find information on Divided families? Did they find the right page independently?	☐ L2 not attained ☐ Low 2 ☐ Secure 2 ☐ High 2
AF5 Some effective language choices noted	Ask the child to find words that are related to this topic. Ask them if they know what the words mean.		Was the child able to find specialised vocabulary? e.g. 'barrage balloons' (p6), 'Blitz' (p10).	☐ L2 not attained ☐ Low 2 ☐ Secure 2 ☐ High 2
AF6 Simple statements about likes and dislikes in reading, sometimes with reasons	Discuss the illustrations in this book. Ask the child to find drawings, photographs and posters. Ask them to say which ones are helpful in showing us what the war was like.		Was the child able to express an opinion on the best way to illustrate this topic? Could they say why a particular illustration was useful or effective?	☐ L2 not attained ☐ Low 2 ☐ Secure 2 ☐ High 2
AF7 General features of a few text types identified	Look at the cover and ask the child to say whether this looks like a story or an information book. Ask them to say what they look for when deciding whether a book is fiction or non-fiction.		Note the features that the child lists when distinguishing between fact and fiction, e.g. do they mention: chapters/topic headings, drawings/photographs, diagrams, title, blurb, contents list?	☐ L2 not attained ☐ Low 2 ☐ Secure 2 ☐ High 2

© Oxford University Press: 2010 Copying permitted within purchasing school only

Writing assessment

Read and discuss 'Evacuation' on pages 8–9. Ask the child to imagine that they were evacuated in wartime to live with another family. Talk about the kind of houses they may have stayed in and the people they might have gone to stay with. Ask them to suggest three or four chapter headings to cover topics such as arrival, going to school, new friends and going home. Ask them to write the text independently.

Use the chart below to help you gather information from this piece of writing to assess children's attainment against the Writing Assessment Focuses at Level 2.

Level 2 Assessment Focus guidelines	Notes on child's writing	Ideas for following up child's writing	Best fit NC Level
AF1 Mostly relevant ideas and content, sometimes repetitive or sparse		Does the text consistently describe the experience of an evacuated child?	☐ L2 not attained ☐ Low 2 ☐ Secure 2 ☐ High 2
AF2 Some basic purpose established, e.g. main features of story		Are events, characters and setting briefly described?	☐ L2 not attained ☐ Low 2 ☐ Secure 2 ☐ High 2
AF3 Some basic sequencing of ideas or material		Are there chapter headings and a clear beginning, middle and end?	☐ L2 not attained ☐ Low 2 ☐ Secure 2 ☐ High 2
AF4 Ideas in sections grouped by content, some linking by simple pronouns		Do the events follow a logical sequence? Are pronouns used correctly?	☐ L2 not attained ☐ Low 2 ☐ Secure 2 ☐ High 2
AF5 Mainly simple sentences with 'and' used to connect clauses		Does the child use 'and' as a connective? Are any other connectives used?	☐ L2 not attained ☐ Low 2 ☐ Secure 2 ☐ High 2
AF6 Sentence demarcation with capital letters and full stops usually accurate; Clause structure mostly grammatically correct		Does the child use capital letters and full stops correctly? Was the order of words and phrases in sentences correct? Did sentences make sense?	☐ L2 not attained ☐ Low 2 ☐ Secure 2 ☐ High 2
AF7 Some adventurous word choices, e.g. opportune use of new vocabulary		Does the child use the new vocabulary they have learned from the book? Are these words used appropriately?	☐ L2 not attained ☐ Low 2 ☐ Secure 2 ☐ High 2
AF8 Usually correct spelling of high frequency grammatical function words		Are high frequency words spelled accurately?	☐ L2 not attained ☐ Low 2 ☐ Secure 2 ☐ High 2

Assessment Pointers for Stage 11/National Curriculum Level 3 (based on Stage 11 *Non-fiction War Children*)

Reading assessment

Use the chart below to help you gather information to assess children's attainment against the Reading Assessment Focuses at Level 3.

Level 3 Assessment Focus guidelines	Suggested prompt	Notes on child's response	Ideas for following up child's response	Best fit NC Level
AF1 Range of strategies used mostly effectively to read with fluency, understanding and expression	Ask the child to read the memories in the speech bubbles on pages 7–11.		Does the child maintain a fluent pace in their reading? Do they engage with the emotions described and read accordingly? Can they explain words such as 'trenches' and 'ordeal'?	☐ L3 not attained ☐ Low 3 ☐ Secure 3 ☐ High 3
AF2 Some comments include quotations from or references to the text, but not always relevant	Read pages 4 and 5, then ask: *Why did the war begin? Why did people die? When did the war end?* Ask them to show you the evidence.		Does the child answer the questions you asked, or give other information? Can they find the evidence to support their answers?	☐ L3 not attained ☐ Low 3 ☐ Secure 3 ☐ High 3
AF3 Responses to text show meaning established at a literal level, or based on personal speculation; Straightforward inference based on a single point of reference in the text	After reading pages 6–13, ask the child to explain what they think life was like for children at this time. What made children sad or happy? What was 'evacuation'? Read pages 14 and 15, then ask the child to explain what is meant by the Holocaust.		Has the child made deductions about children living at this time? Are their ideas based on the text or on a personal response? Does the child use the text box on page 14 or the entry in the Glossary to give a definition? Do they talk about these pages without defining the term?	☐ L3 not attained ☐ Low 3 ☐ Secure 3 ☐ High 3
AF4 A few basic features of organisation at text level identified, with little or no linked comment	Ask the child to talk about the way the text is presented. Scan through the book and ask them to name all the ways that the book gives us information.		Can the child identify and name: headings, illustrations, captions, text boxes, speech bubbles, posters, photographs, quotations, index, glossary, contents page? Can they say how any particular feature makes information easy to find?	☐ L3 not attained ☐ Low 3 ☐ Secure 3 ☐ High 3
AF5 A few basic features of writer's use of language identified, with little or no comment	Ask the child to look through pages 4–9 to discover questions used by the author in headings. Ask: *Do the questions help you find information?*		Can the child find the answer to each question? Can they think of a question for a heading for the first paragraph on page 8? How would a question help a reader find information?	☐ L3 not attained ☐ Low 3 ☐ Secure 3 ☐ High 3
AF6 Express personal response but with little awareness of writer's viewpoint or effect on reader	Read pages 12 and 13. Ask the child to explain 'Divided families'. Ask: *How did families become divided? What did the author of the letter on page 13 think about the war?*		Has the child understood all the ways that families were split up at this time? Can they identify the feelings of the letter writer? Can they suggest the feelings of mothers and fathers?	☐ L3 not attained ☐ Low 3 ☐ Secure 3 ☐ High 3
AF7 Recognition of some features of the context of texts	Ask: *When did everything in this book happen? Do you know anyone who was alive during the war? Do you know when your grandparents were born?*		Check that the child has some idea about the length of time since 1940 in terms of generations, e.g. grandparents or great grandparents.	☐ L3 not attained ☐ Low 3 ☐ Secure 3 ☐ High 3

© Oxford University Press: 2010 Copying permitted within purchasing school only

Writing assessment

Read and discuss 'Evacuation' on pages 8–9. Ask the child to write an account of the World War 2 evacuation scheme in their own words, using questions as paragraph headings, e.g. Why were children evacuated in wartime? Where did they go? Who looked after the children? Who enjoyed being evacuated? Who didn't like being evacuated? Then ask them to write a conclusion saying what they would have liked or disliked about being evacuated.

Use the chart below to help you gather information from this piece of writing to assess children's attainment against the Writing Assessment Focuses at Level 3.

Level 3 Assessment Focus guidelines	Notes on child's writing	Ideas for following up child's writing	Best fit NC Level
AF1 Some appropriate ideas and content included; Some attempt to elaborate on basic information or events		Does the information in each paragraph answer the question in the heading? Does the child use their own vocabulary to make it interesting to read?	☐ L3 not attained ☐ Low 3 ☐ Secure 3 ☐ High 3
AF2 Purpose established at a general level; Main features of selected form sometimes signalled to reader; Some attempts at appropriate style, with attention to reader		Does the child use a style that's broadly appropriate to a non-chronological report? Do they stick to the headings or get side-tracked into irrelevant information?	☐ L3 not attained ☐ Low 3 ☐ Secure 3 ☐ High 3
AF3 Some attempt to organise ideas; Openings and closings usually signalled; Some attempt to sequence ideas or material logically		Does the answer to the first question set the scene and say when the events happened? Does the personal statement at the end form a conclusion to the report?	☐ L3 not attained ☐ Low 3 ☐ Secure 3 ☐ High 3
AF4 Some internal structure within sections of text; Within paragraphs/structures, some links between sentences; Movement between paragraphs/sections sometimes abrupt or disjointed		Do the answers to the questions show that the child has a coherent grasp of the subject? Do the sentences follow logically, or are they simply a list of facts from the book?	☐ L3 not attained ☐ Low 3 ☐ Secure 3 ☐ High 3
AF5 Reliance mainly on simply structured sentences; 'and', 'but', 'so' are the most common connectives, subordination occasionally; Some limited variation in use of tense and verb forms, not always secure		Is there some variety in the use of connectives? Do they use the past tense consistently?	☐ L3 not attained ☐ Low 3 ☐ Secure 3 ☐ High 3
AF6 Straightforward sentences usually demarcated accurately with full stops, capital letters, question and exclamation marks; Some, limited, use of speech punctuation		Does the child use a range of final sentence punctuation correctly? Are some commas used correctly in longer sentences?	☐ L3 not attained ☐ Low 3 ☐ Secure 3 ☐ High 3
AF7 Simple, generally appropriate vocabulary used; Some words selected for effect or occasion		Does the child use the specialised vocabulary related to the war? Are these words used appropriately? Do they sometimes use interesting words of their own choice?	☐ L3 not attained ☐ Low 3 ☐ Secure 3 ☐ High 3
AF8 Correct spelling of: some common grammatical function words; common content/lexical words with more than one morpheme, including compound words		Does the child make phonetically plausible attempts to spell tricky words? Have they referred to the book to spell specialised words? Are there spelling patterns that need practice?	☐ L3 not attained ☐ Low 3 ☐ Secure 3 ☐ High 3

Assessment Pointers for Stage 12/National Curriculum Level 3 (based on Stage 12 Playscripts *The Lie Detector*)

Reading assessment

Use the chart below to help you gather information to assess children's attainment against the Reading Assessment Focuses at Level 3.

Level 3 Assessment Focus guidelines	Suggested prompt	Notes on child's response	Ideas for following up child's response	Best fit NC Level
AF1 Range of strategies used mostly effectively to read with fluency, understanding and expression	Ask the child to read Laura's speech on pages 4–5 aloud.		Does the child read fluently and expressively, taking note of the sentence punctuation and other clues in the text to make their reading sound natural?	☐ L3 not attained ☐ Low 3 ☐ Secure 3 ☐ High 3
AF2 Some comments include quotations from or references to the text, but not always relevant	Read pages 14–21, and then ask: *Does Harry believe Laura? Is it really true about the lie detector? How do you know?*		Does the child answer the questions you asked, or give other information? Can they find the evidence to support their answers?	☐ L3 not attained ☐ Low 3 ☐ Secure 3 ☐ High 3
AF3 Straightforward inference based on a single point of reference in the text	Read pages 22 and 23, then ask the child how they think Dad feels about Laura's behaviour.		Can the child infer that Dad is not pleased with Laura because she has been lying? Can they point to evidence for this in the text? e.g. 'I don't think Harry found it very funny.'	☐ L3 not attained ☐ Low 3 ☐ Secure 3 ☐ High 3
AF4 A few basic features of organisation at text level identified, with little or no linked comment	Ask the child to talk about the way the text is presented. Scan through the book and ask them to pick out all of the playscript features they can.		Can the child identify and name stage directions, character names and scene headings? Can they describe how the speech is set out differently in a playscript?	☐ L3 not attained ☐ Low 3 ☐ Secure 3 ☐ High 3
AF5 A few basic features of writer's use of language identified, but with little or no comment	Ask the child to look through pages 28 and 29 to find some places where the author has used language that sounds like real speech.		Can the child identify specific parts of the text that sound like speech (e.g. abbreviations like 'Course' instead of 'Of course', or the use of very short sentences)?	☐ L3 not attained ☐ Low 3 ☐ Secure 3 ☐ High 3
AF6 Express personal response but with little awareness of writer's viewpoint or effect on reader	At the end of the play, ask: *Why do you think Laura doesn't want the lie detector any more? Do you think the author is trying to give us a message with this play?*		Is the child able to understand why Laura might not want the lie detector? Can they identify a possible message in the play (e.g. about friendship and the importance of being kind as well as the importance of telling the truth)?	☐ L3 not attained ☐ Low 3 ☐ Secure 3 ☐ High 3
AF7 Recognition of some features of the context of texts	Ask: *When do you think this play was set?*		Check that the child can tell that the play is set fairly recently. Can they pick up on details such as the references to new video players that tell us the action is set a few years ago?	☐ L3 not attained ☐ Low 3 ☐ Secure 3 ☐ High 3

© Oxford University Press: 2010

Copying permitted within purchasing school only

Writing assessment

Reread Scene 4, and then ask the child to write a further short scene for the play. It could be based on the conversation between Gemma and Laura as they walk to Gemma's house. If the child is doing this activity in a group, you could ask the children to discuss it in advance and role play the conversation before they start to write.

Use the chart below to help you gather information from this piece of writing to assess children's attainment against the Writing Assessment Focuses at Level 3.

Level 3 Assessment Focus guidelines	Notes on child's writing	Ideas for following up child's writing	Best fit NC Level
AF1 Some appropriate ideas and content included; Attempt to adopt viewpoint, though often not maintained or consistent		Is the content of the child's extra scene appropriate to the rest of the play? Are they able to relate their new scene back to earlier events in the play? Does the characters' speech reflect their different viewpoints?	☐ L3 not attained ☐ Low 3 ☐ Secure 3 ☐ High 3
AF2 Purpose established at a general level; Main features of selected form sometimes signalled to the reader; Some attempts at appropriate style, with attention to reader		Does the child use a style that's broadly appropriate to a playscript? Are they able to maintain the use of features such as dialogue and stage directions?	☐ L3 not attained ☐ Low 3 ☐ Secure 3 ☐ High 3
AF3 Some attempt to organise ideas with related points; Openings and closings usually signalled; Some attempt to sequence ideas or material logically		Does the scene follow a clear chronological structure? Is it easy for the reader to follow? Is the ending a reasonably satisfying one or does it fizzle out?	☐ L3 not attained ☐ Low 3 ☐ Secure 3 ☐ High 3
AF4 Within paragraphs/sections, some links between sentences		Does the child attempt to make links between the sentences in a speech, and between speeches, e.g. by using connectives and showing how the characters pick up on what each other says?	☐ L3 not attained ☐ Low 3 ☐ Secure 3 ☐ High 3
AF5 Reliance mainly on simply structured sentences; 'and', 'but' and 'so' are the most common connectives, subordination occasionally; Some limited variation in use of tense and verb forms, not always secure		Is there some variety in the use of connectives? Do they use tenses consistently?	☐ L3 not attained ☐ Low 3 ☐ Secure 3 ☐ High 3
AF6 Straightforward sentences usually demarcated accurately with full stops, capital letters, question and exclamation marks		Does the child use a range of final sentence punctuation correctly, including question marks and exclamation marks as well as full stops?	☐ L3 not attained ☐ Low 3 ☐ Secure 3 ☐ High 3
AF7 Simple, generally appropriate vocabulary used, limited in range; Some words selected for effect or occasion		Does the child use appropriate vocabulary for two friends chatting together? Do they sometimes use interesting words of their own choice, where appropriate?	☐ L3 not attained ☐ Low 3 ☐ Secure 3 ☐ High 3
AF8 Correct spelling of: some common grammatical function words; common content/lexical words with more than one morpheme, including compound words		Does the child make phonetically plausible attempts to spell tricky words? Are there spelling patterns that need practice?	☐ L3 not attained ☐ Low 3 ☐ Secure 3 ☐ High 3

Assessment Pointers for Stage 12/National Curriculum Level 4 (based on Stage 12 Playscripts *The Lie Detector*)

Reading assessment

Use the chart below to help you gather information to assess children's attainment against the Reading Assessment Focuses at Level 4.

Level 4 Assessment Focus guidelines	Suggested prompt	Notes on child's response	Ideas for following up child's response	Best fit NC Level
AF2 Some relevant points identified	Ask the child to read Scene 1 and sum up what Laura thinks of Gemma at this point.		Can the child find evidence in more than one place in the scene? Do they understand that Laura thinks Gemma is a liar?	☐ L4 not attained ☐ Low 4 ☐ Secure 4 ☐ High 4
AF3 Comments make inferences based on evidence from different points in the text	Ask the child what Gemma thinks about the lie detector when she first sees it, and what she thinks about it by the end of the play. How do they know?		Can the child identify how Gemma's view of the lie detector changes during the play? Can they find evidence in the text to support their understanding of Gemma's views?	☐ L4 not attained ☐ Low 4 ☐ Secure 4 ☐ High 4
AF4 Some basic features of organisation at text level identified	Ask the child to comment on some of the differences between a playscript and a novel or story.		Encourage the child to make connections between the play and the story (if available). Can they think of any reasons why a playscript is set out differently from a story?	☐ L4 not attained ☐ Low 4 ☐ Secure 4 ☐ High 4
AF5 Some basic features of writer's use of language identified; Simple comments on writer's choices	Ask: *How does the author make it sound as though the characters are really talking? Can you find some examples where it sounds like real speech?*		Encourage the child to explain the reasons why they chose particular examples – e.g. because they contain less formal words that are often used in speech, or because the characters don't always speak in whole sentences.	☐ L4 not attained ☐ Low 4 ☐ Secure 4 ☐ High 4
AF6 Simple comment on overall effect on reader	Ask: *What kind of character do you think Laura is? Do you think she was right to use the lie detector on Gemma? Why or why not?*		Is the child able to give reasons for their opinions of Laura as a character, related to the text?	☐ L4 not attained ☐ Low 4 ☐ Secure 4 ☐ High 4
AF7 Simple comment on the effect that the reader's or writer's context has on the meaning of texts	Ask: *Do you think this playscript is realistic?*		Can the child make links between the play and the events they may have experienced in their own life?	☐ L4 not attained ☐ Low 4 ☐ Secure 4 ☐ High 4

© Oxford University Press: 2010
Copying permitted within purchasing school only

Writing assessment

Ask the child to write another scene for the playscript in which Laura does something particularly nice for Gemma to make up for being nasty to her with the lie detector. Remind them to use playscript features such as stage directions and set out the dialogue as in *The Lie Detector*.

Use the chart below to help you gather information from this piece of writing to assess children's attainment against the Writing Assessment Focuses at Level 4.

Level 4 Assessment Focus guidelines	Notes on child's writing	Ideas for following up child's writing	Best fit NC Level
AF1 Relevant ideas and content chosen; Straightforward viewpoint generally established and maintained		Does the writing follow a coherent storyline? Is the dialogue appropriate for the characters? Are the characters from *The Lie Detector* recognisable?	☐ L4 not attained ☐ Low 4 ☐ Secure 4 ☐ High 4
AF2 Main purpose of writing is clear but not always consistently maintained; Main features of selected form are clear and appropriate to purpose; Style generally appropriate to task, though awareness of reader not always sustained		Does the child use a style that's broadly appropriate to a realistic playscript? Does the dialogue make sense and is it easy to follow? Do they stick to their storyline or wander off on a different track?	☐ L4 not attained ☐ Low 4 ☐ Secure 4 ☐ High 4
AF3 Ideas organised: by clustering related points or by time sequence; simply with a fitting opening and closing, sometimes linked; generally in logical sequence but overall direction of writing not always clearly signalled		Does the child organise the scene so that the reader can understand it? Is there a logical progression? Has the child tried to give the scene an effective opening and ending?	☐ L4 not attained ☐ Low 4 ☐ Secure 4 ☐ High 4
AF4 Some attempts to establish simple links between paragraphs/sections not always maintained		Do the speeches in the scene follow on well from one another? Are there links made between sentences such as connective phrases?	☐ L4 not attained ☐ Low 4 ☐ Secure 4 ☐ High 4
AF5 Some variety in length, structure or subject of sentences; Some variation, generally accurate, in tense and verb forms		Does the child structure and present most of their sentences correctly? Do they use a mixture of shorter and longer sentences to give a speech-like effect?	☐ L4 not attained ☐ Low 4 ☐ Secure 4 ☐ High 4
AF6 Sentences demarcated accurately throughout the text, including question marks; Commas used in lists and occasionally to mark clauses, although not always accurately		Does the child use a range of final sentence punctuation correctly? Are commas used occasionally to show subordinate clauses?	☐ L4 not attained ☐ Low 4 ☐ Secure 4 ☐ High 4
AF7 Some evidence of deliberate vocabulary choices		Does the child use appropriate words to give the effect of direct speech? Do they sometimes use interesting words for particular effects?	☐ L4 not attained ☐ Low 4 ☐ Secure 4 ☐ High 4
AF8 Correct spelling of: most common grammatical function words, including adverbs with '-ly' formation; regularly formed content/lexical words, including those with multiple morphemes; most past and present tense inflections, plurals		Look at any spelling mistakes to assess patterns of error. Are there spelling patterns that need practice?	☐ L4 not attained ☐ Low 4 ☐ Secure 4 ☐ High 4

Assessment Pointers for Stage 13/National Curriculum Level 3 (based on Stage 13 Graphic Novels *The Golden Scarab*)

Reading assessment

Use the chart below to help you gather information to assess children's attainment against the Reading Assessment Focuses at Level 3.

Level 3 Assessment Focus guidelines	Suggested prompt	Notes on child's response	Ideas for following up child's response	Best fit NC Level
AF1 Range of strategies used mostly effectively to read with fluency, understanding and expression	Ask the child to read a section of dialogue using the punctuation and visual clues such as words in bold or capital letters to help them get the tone right. Can they use voices to show the different characters?		Does the child maintain a fluent pace in their reading? Are they able to use clues such as sentence punctuation to help them read with expression?	☐ L3 not attained ☐ Low 3 ☐ Secure 3 ☐ High 3
AF2 Simple, most obvious points identified though there may be some misunderstandings	When the child has read the book ask them to use one of the non-fiction pages to make a link between the main characters and historical events.		Notice whether the child can make links between the names of the characters and the historical figures. Can they work out where and when the story was set?	☐ L3 not attained ☐ Low 3 ☐ Secure 3 ☐ High 3
AF3 Responses to text show meaning established at a literal level, or based on personal speculation; Straightforward inference based on a single point of reference in the text	Ask: *Can you tell me why Pharaoh Akhenaten is in danger?* Ask: *How can you tell that Meri is an important person?*		If necessary focus the child's answer by asking further questions, such as: *Why were the priests angry with the Pharaoh? What gift did they give him? What did the scarab ring do?* Prompt the child to find some evidence in the text (including pictures) to support their view.	☐ L3 not attained ☐ Low 3 ☐ Secure 3 ☐ High 3
AF4 A few basic features of organisation at text level identified, with little or no linked comment	Ask the child to use the Contents page to locate where they could find out more information about Mummies.		Check the child understands what chapter headings and Time Out headings are. Talk about how they help the reader make predictions about the chapter or Time Out section and find their way around the book.	☐ L3 not attained ☐ Low 3 ☐ Secure 3 ☐ High 3
AF5 A few basic features of writer's use of language identified, but with little or no comment	Ask: *How can you tell that the man holding Layla (on page 7) is lying?*		Ask the child to use the pictures as well as the words to help them make their judgements about the man. If necessary, draw their attention to how his story changes. Ask them to consider if an animal would be a good judge of character.	☐ L3 not attained ☐ Low 3 ☐ Secure 3 ☐ High 3
AF6 Express personal response but with little awareness of writer's viewpoint or effect on reader	Ask: *Which characters did you like? Were there any that you thought behaved badly?*		Can the child give some reasons why they liked or disliked some characters? Did the pictures help them make up their minds? If so, how?	☐ L3 not attained ☐ Low 3 ☐ Secure 3 ☐ High 3
AF7 Recognition of some features of the context of texts	Can the child identify which parts of the book are fiction and non-fiction?		Check the child can see the difference in layout and content of the graphic novel and non-fiction aspects of the book.	☐ L3 not attained ☐ Low 3 ☐ Secure 3 ☐ High 3

© Oxford University Press: 2010   Copying permitted within purchasing school only

Writing assessment

Ask the child to write another episode of the story about Princess Meri and Layla. Suggest that the characters visit the tomb that is being constructed for the Pharaoh and have an exciting encounter there. Remind the child to describe the setting and include dialogue in their writing.

Use the chart below to help you gather information from this piece of writing to assess children's attainment against the Writing Assessment Focuses at Level 3.

Level 3 Assessment Focus guidelines	Notes on child's writing	Ideas for following up child's writing	Best fit NC Level
AF1 Some appropriate ideas and content included; Some attempt to elaborate on basic information or events		Does the writing follow a broadly coherent story? Is the description of the setting appropriate? Is the story structured with a beginning, middle and end?	☐ L3 not attained ☐ Low 3 ☐ Secure 3 ☐ High 3
AF2 Purpose established at a general level; Main features of selected form sometimes signalled to the reader; Some attempts at appropriate style, with attention to reader		Does the child use a style that's broadly appropriate to an adventure story? Do they stick to their storyline or wander off on a different track?	☐ L3 not attained ☐ Low 3 ☐ Secure 3 ☐ High 3
AF3 Some attempt to organise ideas with related points; Openings and closings usually signalled; Some attempt to sequence ideas or material logically		Does the child organise the story so that the reader can understand it, e.g. by sticking to chronological order?	☐ L3 not attained ☐ Low 3 ☐ Secure 3 ☐ High 3
AF4 Some internal structure within sections of text; Within paragraphs/sections, some links between sentences; Movement between paragraphs/sections sometimes abrupt or disjointed		Does the child use paragraphs, or group related ideas together within the story? Do they use some pronouns and/or adverbials to link sentences?	☐ L3 not attained ☐ Low 3 ☐ Secure 3 ☐ High 3
AF5 Reliance mainly on simply structured sentences; 'and', 'but', 'so' are the most common connectives, subordination occasionally; Some limited variation in use of tense and verb forms, not always secure		Does the child structure and present most of their sentences correctly? Do they use simple connectives and verb forms correctly?	☐ L3 not attained ☐ Low 3 ☐ Secure 3 ☐ High 3
AF6 Straightforward sentences usually demarcated accurately with full stops, capital letters, question and exclamation marks; Some, limited, use of speech punctuation		Does the child use a range of final sentence punctuation correctly? Do they attempt to punctuate direct speech?	☐ L3 not attained ☐ Low 3 ☐ Secure 3 ☐ High 3
AF7 Simple, generally appropriate vocabulary used, limited in range; Some words selected for effect or occasion		Does the child usually use appropriate words? Do they sometimes use interesting words for particular effects? Have they used words that describe Ancient Egyptian life?	☐ L3 not attained ☐ Low 3 ☐ Secure 3 ☐ High 3
AF8 Correct spelling of: some common grammatical function words; common content/lexical words with more than one morpheme, including compound words		Does the child make phonetically plausible attempts to spell tricky words? Look at any spelling mistakes to assess patterns of error. Are there spelling patterns that need practice?	☐ L3 not attained ☐ Low 3 ☐ Secure 3 ☐ High 3

© Oxford University Press: 2010

Assessment Pointers for Stage 13/National Curriculum Level 4 (based on Stage 13 Graphic Novels *The Golden Scarab*)

Reading assessment

Use the chart below to help you gather information to assess children's attainment against the Reading Assessment Focuses at Level 4.

Level 4 Assessment Focus guidelines	Suggested prompt	Notes on child's response	Ideas for following up child's response	Best fit NC Level
AF2 Some relevant points identified	Ask the child to summarise the whole story as briefly as possible.		Can the child pick out the most important points of the story, or do they attempt to retell it all in detail?	☐ L4 not attained ☐ Low 4 ☐ Secure 4 ☐ High 4
AF3 Comments make inferences based on evidence from different points in the text	Ask: *What kind of person is Pharaoh Akhenaten?*		Encourage the child to refer to evidence from more than one place in the text. If necessary, focus the child's answer by asking further questions, such as: *How does he talk? What do other characters think of him and how do they behave towards him? How does he treat other people?*	☐ L4 not attained ☐ Low 4 ☐ Secure 4 ☐ High 4
AF4 Some basic features of organisation at text level identified	Ask the child to comment on the timeline in the introduction.		Encourage the child to make connections between the timelines and the story. Ask them to consider how this way of representing historical information is helpful to the reader.	☐ L4 not attained ☐ Low 4 ☐ Secure 4 ☐ High 4
AF5 Some basic features of writer's use of language identified, with little comment; Simple comments on writer's choices	Ask the child to find a passage in the book that they think is particularly exciting. Ask: *How does the writer try to make it exciting for the reader?*		Encourage the child to think about the vocabulary used, the use of bold text, capitals, etc., and the effect of the artwork in building up the excitement.	☐ L4 not attained ☐ Low 4 ☐ Secure 4 ☐ High 4
AF6 Simple comment on overall effect on reader	Ask: *How would you describe the main characters Princess Meri, Layla, the Pharaoh and his wife? Did you like them? Why, or why not?*		Is the child able to briefly sum up what each character is like and state a personal response to the characters? Can they give a simple reason for their views?	☐ L4 not attained ☐ Low 4 ☐ Secure 4 ☐ High 4
AF7 Simple comment on the effect that the reader's or writer's context has on the meaning of texts	Ask: *Do you think you need to know anything about Ancient Egypt in order to understand this story?*		Can the child identify any aspects of the story that might be puzzling to people who didn't know anything about Ancient Egypt? Can they point out ways in which the book helps the reader learn about this historical period?	☐ L4 not attained ☐ Low 4 ☐ Secure 4 ☐ High 4

© Oxford University Press: 2010   Copying permitted within purchasing school only

Writing assessment

Ask the child to write another episode of the story about Princess Meri and Layla. Suggest that they visit the tomb that is being constructed for the Pharaoh and have an exciting encounter there. Remind them to describe the setting and include dialogue in their writing.

Use the chart below to help you gather information from this piece of writing to assess children's attainment against the Writing Assessment Focuses at Level 4.

Level 4 Assessment Focus guidelines	Notes on child's writing	Ideas for following up child's writing	Best fit NC Level
AF1 Relevant ideas and content chosen; Some ideas and material developed in detail		Does the child use ideas that fit with a story set in Ancient Egypt? Have they attempted a strong storyline, with a beginning, a middle and an end, and attempted to develop the plot during the course of the story?	☐ L4 not attained ☐ Low 4 ☐ Secure 4 ☐ High 4
AF2 Main purpose of writing is clear but not always consistently maintained; Main features of selected form are clear and appropriate to purpose; Style generally appropriate to task, though awareness of reader not always sustained		Does the child use a style that's appropriate to an adventure story? Is the story written in the past tense and in chronological order? Have they managed to make the story understandable to the reader?	☐ L4 not attained ☐ Low 4 ☐ Secure 4 ☐ High 4
AF3 Ideas organised: by clustering related points or by time sequence; simply with a fitting opening and closing, sometimes linked; generally in logical sequence but overall direction of writing not always clearly signalled		Is there a logical progression through the story? Has the child tried to give the story an exciting opening and a satisfying ending?	☐ L4 not attained ☐ Low 4 ☐ Secure 4 ☐ High 4
AF4 Paragraphs/sections help to organise content; Within paragraphs/sections, limited range of connections between sentences; Some attempts to establish simple links between paragraphs/sections not always maintained		Does the child use paragraphs, or group related ideas together within the story? Are there links made between sentences or between paragraphs, such as connective phrases, pronouns and adverbials?	☐ L4 not attained ☐ Low 4 ☐ Secure 4 ☐ High 4
AF5 Some variety in length, structure or subject of sentences; Use of some subordinating connectives; Some variation, generally accurate, in tense and verb forms		Does the child sometimes vary the length of sentences? Do they use simple connectives and verb forms correctly? If different tenses are used (e.g. in narrative and in direct speech) does the child mostly handle this correctly?	☐ L4 not attained ☐ Low 4 ☐ Secure 4 ☐ High 4
AF6 Sentences demarcated accurately throughout the text, including question marks; Speech marks to denote speech generally accurate, with some other speech punctuation; Commas used in lists and occasionally to mark clauses, although not always accurately		Does the child use a range of final sentence punctuation correctly? Do they use speech marks accurately to mark out direct speech? Are commas sometimes used accurately?	☐ L4 not attained ☐ Low 4 ☐ Secure 4 ☐ High 4
AF7 Some evidence of deliberate vocabulary choices; Some expansion of general vocabulary to match topic		Does the child use vocabulary in a way that shows they know the meaning of the words? Do they sometimes use interesting words for particular effects? Have they used specialist words, where appropriate, to describe aspects of Ancient Egyptian life, e.g. words gained from their reading?	☐ L4 not attained ☐ Low 4 ☐ Secure 4 ☐ High 4
AF8 Correct spelling of: most common grammatical function words, including adverbs with '-ly' formation; regularly formed content/ lexical words, including those with multiple morphemes; most past and present tense inflections, plurals		Look at any spelling mistakes to assess patterns of error. Are there spelling patterns that need practice?	☐ L4 not attained ☐ Low 4 ☐ Secure 4 ☐ High 4

Assessment Pointers for Stage 14/National Curriculum Level 3 (based on Stage 14 Classics *The Secret Garden*)

Reading assessment

Use the chart below to help you gather information to assess children's attainment against the Reading Assessment Focuses at Level 3.

Level 3 Assessment Focus guidelines	Suggested prompt	Notes on child's response	Ideas for following up child's response	Best fit NC Level
AF1 Range of strategies used mostly effectively to read with fluency, understanding and expression	Encourage the child to read aloud a passage with dialogue, such as Chapter 5, in which Mary meets Dickon.		Does the child maintain a fluent pace in their reading? Are they able to use clues such as sentence punctuation to help them read with expression? Are they able to attempt Dickon's dialogue, which is in dialect?	☐ L3 not attained ☐ Low 3 ☐ Secure 3 ☐ High 3
AF2 Simple, most obvious points identified though there may be some misunderstandings	When the child has read the book, ask them to explain why the garden was so important to the story.		Notice whether the child can identify some of the reasons why the garden is important to the characters.	☐ L3 not attained ☐ Low 3 ☐ Secure 3 ☐ High 3
AF3 Straightforward inference based on a single point of reference in the text	Ask: *How can you tell that Mary was lonely?*		Prompt the child to find some evidence in the text to support their view.	☐ L3 not attained ☐ Low 3 ☐ Secure 3 ☐ High 3
AF4 A few basic features of organisation at text level identified, with little or no linked comment	Ask the child to use the chapter titles on the Contents page to predict which chapter will be the most exciting.		Encourage the child to visualise what the chapter titles might be about. Can they make some basic predictions based on the titles?	☐ L3 not attained ☐ Low 3 ☐ Secure 3 ☐ High 3
AF5 A few basic features of writer's use of language identified, with little or no comment	Ask: *How does the author show us that Dickon and Martha are different from Colin and Mary?*		Draw the child's attention to how the children speak differently.	☐ L3 not attained ☐ Low 3 ☐ Secure 3 ☐ High 3
AF6 Express personal response but with little awareness of writer's viewpoint or effect on reader	Ask: *Which characters did you like? Were there any that you thought behaved badly?*		Can the child give some reasons why they liked or disliked some characters?	☐ L3 not attained ☐ Low 3 ☐ Secure 3 ☐ High 3
AF7 Recognition of some features of the context of texts	Can the child identify which parts of the book took place in India and which parts took place in the Yorkshire Moors?		Look at the text in italics before the first chapter and talk about how and why Mary has to move from India to Yorkshire. Why does the child think the first bit of text is in italics?	☐ L3 not attained ☐ Low 3 ☐ Secure 3 ☐ High 3

© Oxford University Press: 2010   Copying permitted within purchasing school only

Writing assessment

Ask the child to write as Mary (in the first person) describing the night she met Colin. Tell them to make their retelling of walking down the corridors in the dim candlelight as exciting as possible.

Use the chart below to help you gather information from this piece of writing to assess children's attainment against the Writing Assessment Focuses at Level 3.

Level 3 Assessment Focus guidelines	Notes on child's writing	Ideas for following up child's writing	Best fit NC Level
AF1 Some appropriate ideas and content included; Some attempt to elaborate on basic information or events		Does the child's writing follow a broadly coherent story? Does it include some description of the setting?	☐ L3 not attained ☐ Low 3 ☐ Secure 3 ☐ High 3
AF2 Purpose established at a general level; Main features of selected form sometimes signalled to the reader; Some attempts at appropriate style, with attention to reader		Does the child use a style that's broadly appropriate to a spooky story? Do they stick to their storyline or wander off on a different track?	☐ L3 not attained ☐ Low 3 ☐ Secure 3 ☐ High 3
AF3 Some attempt to organise ideas with related points; Openings and closings usually signalled; Some attempt to sequence ideas or material logically		Does the child organise the story so that the reader can understand it, e.g. by sticking to chronological order?	☐ L3 not attained ☐ Low 3 ☐ Secure 3 ☐ High 3
AF4 Some internal structure within text; Within paragraphs/sections, some links between sentences; Movement between paragraphs/sections sometimes abrupt or disjointed		Does the child use paragraphs, or group related ideas together within the story? Do they use some pronouns and/or adverbials to link sentences?	☐ L3 not attained ☐ Low 3 ☐ Secure 3 ☐ High 3
AF5 Reliance mainly on simply structured sentences; 'and', 'but', 'so' are the most common connectives, subordination occasionally; Some limited variation in use of tense and verb forms, not always secure		Does the child structure and present most of their sentences correctly? Do they use simple connectives and verb forms correctly?	☐ L3 not attained ☐ Low 3 ☐ Secure 3 ☐ High 3
AF6 Straightforward sentences usually demarcated accurately with full stops, capital letters, question and exclamation marks; Some, limited, use of speech punctuation		Does the child use a range of final sentence punctuation correctly? Do they attempt to punctuate direct speech?	☐ L3 not attained ☐ Low 3 ☐ Secure 3 ☐ High 3
AF7 Simple, generally appropriate vocabulary used; Some words selected for effect or occasion		Does the child use straightforward vocabulary correctly? Do they sometimes use interesting words for particular effects?	☐ L3 not attained ☐ Low 3 ☐ Secure 3 ☐ High 3
AF8 Correct spelling of: some common grammatical function words; common content/lexical words with more than one morpheme, including compound words		Does the child make phonetically plausible attempts to spell tricky words? Look at any spelling mistakes to assess patterns of error. Are there spelling patterns that need practice?	☐ L3 not attained ☐ Low 3 ☐ Secure 3 ☐ High 3

Assessment Pointers for Stage 14/National Curriculum Level 4 (based on Stage 14 Classics *The Secret Garden*)

Reading assessment

Use the chart below to help you gather information to assess children's attainment against the Reading Assessment Focuses at Level 4.

Level 4 Assessment Focus guidelines	Suggested prompt	Notes on child's response	Ideas for following up child's response	Best fit NC Level
AF2 Comments supported by some generally relevant textual reference or quotation	When the child has read the book, ask them to explain why the garden was so important to the story.		Notice whether the child can make a connection between the garden and how the characters change by going there. Do they refer to the text, showing how one or more of the characters is changed by their experiences in the garden?	☐ L4 not attained ☐ Low 4 ☐ Secure 4 ☐ High 4
AF3 Comments make inferences based on evidence from different points in the text	Ask: *Why do you think Colin was kept hidden and in bed?*		In their answers, does the child bear in mind how Mr Craven behaves, his sad history and how he treats his son? Can they make a plausible explanation using these or other clues from the text?	☐ L4 not attained ☐ Low 4 ☐ Secure 4 ☐ High 4
AF4 Some basic features of organisation at text level identified	Ask the child how the author has divided the text up. Why do they think the author chose to do this?		Does the child appreciate that the text is organised into chapters? Can they think of a possible reason for doing this?	☐ L4 not attained ☐ Low 4 ☐ Secure 4 ☐ High 4
AF5 Some basic features of writer's use of language identified	Ask: *Can you find any clues in the language that tell us this story is set in the past?*		Encourage the child to look particularly at the way the different characters speak and at any words that might not be in common use any more. Can they find at least one section of vocabulary that shows the story is not set nowadays?	☐ L4 not attained ☐ Low 4 ☐ Secure 4 ☐ High 4
AF6 Simple comment on overall effect on reader	Ask: *Do you think* The Secret Garden *is a good title for this book?*		Can the child give a simple explanation of why they like or dislike the title?	☐ L4 not attained ☐ Low 4 ☐ Secure 4 ☐ High 4
AF7 Simple comment on the effect that the reader's or writer's context has on the meaning of texts	Ask: *Do you think this story is realistic?*		Can the child make links between the story and their understanding of Victorian Britain?	☐ L4 not attained ☐ Low 4 ☐ Secure 4 ☐ High 4

© Oxford University Press: 2010   Copying permitted within purchasing school only

Writing assessment

Ask the child to write as Mary (in the first person) describing the night she met Colin. Ask them to make their retelling of walking down the corridors with just a dim candlelight as exciting as possible. Remind them to use description to create a spooky atmosphere. Suggest they end their retelling with Mary scurrying back to her room.

Use the chart below to help you gather information from this piece of writing to assess children's attainment against the Writing Assessment Focuses at Level 4.

Level 4 Assessment Focus guidelines	Notes on child's writing	Ideas for following up child's writing	Best fit NC Level
AF1 Relevant ideas and content chosen; Some ideas and material developed in detail		Does the writing follow a coherent storyline? Is the description of the setting and atmosphere appropriate? Are the relevant characters involved, and are they recognisable?	☐ L4 not attained ☐ Low 4 ☐ Secure 4 ☐ High 4
AF2 Main purpose of writing is clear but not always consistently maintained; Main features of selected form are clear and appropriate to purpose; Style generally appropriate to task, though awareness of reader not always sustained		Does the child use a style that's broadly appropriate to a suspense story? Do they make attempts to use language to create a suspenseful atmosphere?	☐ L4 not attained ☐ Low 4 ☐ Secure 4 ☐ High 4
AF3 Ideas organised: by clustering related points or by time sequence; simply with a fitting opening and closing, sometimes linked; generally in logical sequence but overall direction of writing not always clearly signalled		Is there a logical progression through the story? Are time connectives used? Has the child attempted to use an effective beginning and ending?	☐ L4 not attained ☐ Low 4 ☐ Secure 4 ☐ High 4
AF4 Paragraphs/sections help to organise content; Within paragraphs/sections, limited range of connections between sentences; Some attempts to establish simple links between paragraphs/sections not always maintained		Does the child use paragraphs, or group related ideas together within the story? Are links made between sentences and between paragraphs, such as connective phrases?	☐ L4 not attained ☐ Low 4 ☐ Secure 4 ☐ High 4
AF5 Some variety in length, structure and subject of sentences; Use of some subordinating connectives; Some variation, generally accurate, in tense and verb forms		Does the child vary the length of some of the sentences? Do they use subordinating connectives such as 'because'? Where appropriate, do they use different tenses (e.g. in narrative and in dialogue)?	☐ L4 not attained ☐ Low 4 ☐ Secure 4 ☐ High 4
AF6 Sentences demarcated accurately throughout the text, including question marks; Speech marks to denote speech generally accurate, with some other speech punctuation; Commas used in lists and occasionally to mark clauses, although not always accurately		Does the child use a range of final sentence punctuation correctly? Do they use speech marks when writing dialogue? Are commas used in lists and occasionally to show subordinate clauses?	☐ L4 not attained ☐ Low 4 ☐ Secure 4 ☐ High 4
AF7 Some evidence of deliberate vocabulary choices; Some expansion of general vocabulary to match topic		Does the child use appropriate words in the characters' dialogue and thoughts, e.g. words taken from their reading? Do they use effective words to describe the darkness that creates a spooky atmosphere?	☐ L4 not attained ☐ Low 4 ☐ Secure 4 ☐ High 4
AF8 Correct spelling of: most common grammatical function words, including adverbs with '-ly' formation; regularly formed content/lexical words, including those with multiple morphemes; most past and present tense inflections, plurals		Look at any spelling mistakes to assess patterns of error. Are there spelling patterns that need practice?	☐ L4 not attained ☐ Low 4 ☐ Secure 4 ☐ High 4

© Oxford University Press: 2010

Copying permitted within purchasing school only

Assessment Pointers for Stage 15/National Curriculum Level 4 (based on Stage 15 Non-fiction Pirates)

Reading assessment

Use the chart below to help you gather information to assess children's attainment against the Reading Assessment Focuses at Level 4.

Level 4 Assessment Focus guidelines	Suggested prompt	Notes on child's response	Ideas for following up child's response	Best fit NC Level
AF2 Comments supported by some generally relevant textual reference or quotation	When the child has read the book, ask them to explain why they would or wouldn't like to be a pirate.		Notice whether the child can make links with the text and give examples of why life as a pirate would be good or not.	☐ L4 not attained ☐ Low 4 ☐ Secure 4 ☐ High 4
AF3 Inferences often correct, but comments are not always rooted securely in the text or repeat narrative or content	Ask: *Was Francis Drake really a pirate?*		Prompt the child to find some evidence in the text to support their view.	☐ L4 not attained ☐ Low 4 ☐ Secure 4 ☐ High 4
AF4 Some basic features of organisation at text level identified	Ask the child to use the Index to locate where they can find out about Vikings.		Does the child use alphabetical order to help locate the Vikings in the index?	☐ L4 not attained ☐ Low 4 ☐ Secure 4 ☐ High 4
AF5 Some basic features of writer's use of language identified; simple comments on writer's choices	Read page 19 and ask: *How does the author make the captured sailor's terrible ordeal come to life?*		Can the child identify ways in which the writer has made this text vivid, e.g. through word choices?	☐ L4 not attained ☐ Low 4 ☐ Secure 4 ☐ High 4
AF6 Simple comment on overall effect on reader	Ask the child to say which is their favourite pirate and explain why.		Can the child explain how the text appealed to them? Is it the illustrations, pictures or information that made that particular pirate interesting?	☐ L4 not attained ☐ Low 4 ☐ Secure 4 ☐ High 4
AF7 Features common to different texts identified, with simple comment	Give the child a couple of other non-fiction books, such as an instructional text and an explanation. Can they find some differences and similarities between this book and the other non-fiction texts?		Can the child look beyond the differences in subject matter to see the common features, e.g. use of headings to structure the text, use of photographs, etc.?	☐ L4 not attained ☐ Low 4 ☐ Secure 4 ☐ High 4

© Oxford University Press: 2010

Copying permitted within purchasing school only

Writing assessment

Ask the child to write a diary entry in role as a sailor who is captured by pirates and made to take the Pirate's Oath and become a member of the crew. Remind them to write in the past tense and first person, and describe how they felt and what they saw and did on their first day as a pirate.

Use the chart below to help you gather information from this piece of writing to assess children's attainment against the Writing Assessment Focuses at Level 4.

Level 4 Assessment Focus guidelines	Notes on child's writing	Ideas for following up child's writing	Best fit NC Level
AF1 Relevant ideas and content chosen; Some ideas and material developed in detail		Are the ship and other appropriate characters described? Does the diary include details of how the writer feels and what they think?	☐ L4 not attained ☐ Low 4 ☐ Secure 4 ☐ High 4
AF2 Main purpose of writing is clear but not always consistently maintained; Main features of selected form are clear and appropriate to purpose; Style generally appropriate to task, though awareness of reader not always sustained		Is the diary chronologically structured in the past tense, first person with a personal tone? Does the diary recount the first day of the captured sailor as a pirate or does it wander off?	☐ L4 not attained ☐ Low 4 ☐ Secure 4 ☐ High 4
AF3 Ideas organised: by clustering related points or by time sequence; simply with a fitting opening and closing, sometimes linked; generally in logical sequence but overall direction of writing not always clearly signalled		Does the child organise the diary so that the reader can understand it? Is there a logical progression? Are time connectives used?	☐ L4 not attained ☐ Low 4 ☐ Secure 4 ☐ High 4
AF4 Paragraphs/sections help to organise content; Within paragraphs/sections, limited range of connections between sentences; Some attempts to establish simple links between paragraphs/sections not always maintained		Does the child use paragraphs, or group events under headings that show when they happened? Are there links made between sentences and paragraphs, such as connective phrases?	☐ L4 not attained ☐ Low 4 ☐ Secure 4 ☐ High 4
AF5 Some variety in length, structure and subject of sentences; Use of some subordinating connectives		Does the child include sentences of different lengths and with different structures? Do they use subordinating connectives such as 'when'?	☐ L4 not attained ☐ Low 4 ☐ Secure 4 ☐ High 4
AF6 Sentences demarcated accurately throughout the text, including question marks; Speech marks to denote speech generally accurate, with some other speech punctuation; Commas used in lists and occasionally to mark clauses, although not always accurately		Does the child use a range of final sentence punctuation correctly? Do they attempt to punctuate direct speech if it occurs? Are commas used in lists and occasionally to show subordinate clauses?	☐ L4 not attained ☐ Low 4 ☐ Secure 4 ☐ High 4
AF7 Some evidence of deliberate vocabulary choices; Some expansion of general vocabulary to match topic		Does the child use vocabulary in a way that shows they know the meaning of the words? Do they sometimes use interesting words for particular effects? Do they use vocabulary specific to the pirate theme?	☐ L4 not attained ☐ Low 4 ☐ Secure 4 ☐ High 4
AF8 Correct spelling of: most common grammatical function words, including adverbs with '-ly' formation; regularly formed content/lexical words, including those with multiple morphemes; most past and present tense inflections, plurals		Look at any spelling mistakes to assess patterns of error. Are there spelling patterns that need practice?	☐ L4 not attained ☐ Low 4 ☐ Secure 4 ☐ High 4

Assessment Pointers for Stage 15/National Curriculum Level 5 (based on Stage 15 *Non-fiction Pirates*)

Reading assessment

Use the chart below to help you gather information to assess children's attainment against the Reading Assessment Focuses at Level 5.

Level 5 Assessment Focus guidelines	Suggested prompt	Notes on child's response	Ideas for following up child's response	Best fit NC Level
AF2 Comments generally supported by relevant textual reference or quotation, even when points made are not always accurate	Ask the child to choose one of the recount sections in the book and explain in their own words what the chosen recount tells us about being a pirate. Remind them to refer to the text in their answer.		Is the child able to summarise the main points of the recount without simply rereading it? Can they explain their view with reference to the text?	☐ L5 not attained ☐ Low 5 ☐ Secure 5 ☐ High 5
AF3 Comments develop explanation of inferred meanings drawing on evidence across the text	Ask: *How do you think the meaning of the word pirate/piracy has changed over time?*		Can the child make the link between the introduction of the chapter 'Pirate attack', describing romantic perceptions of pirates, and the fictional pirates described in the later chapters? Does the child make a connection between the different forms of piracy described in the book?	☐ L5 not attained ☐ Low 5 ☐ Secure 5 ☐ High 5
AF4 Comments on structural choices show some general awareness of author's craft	Ask: *How does the introduction set the scene for the book?*		Can the children see that the author is setting up connections about pirates that they will explore later on in the book?	☐ L5 not attained ☐ Low 5 ☐ Secure 5 ☐ High 5
AF5 Various features of writer's use of language identified, with some explanation; Comments show some awareness of the effect of writer's language choices	Read page 19. Ask: *How does the author make the captured sailor's terrible ordeal come to life?*		Can the child make connections between the author's description of a sailor being captured and the sailor's own first-hand account?	☐ L5 not attained ☐ Low 5 ☐ Secure 5 ☐ High 5
AF6 General awareness of effect on the reader, with some, often limited, explanation	Ask: *Which of the 'Scourges of the seven seas' (pages 22–25) appealed to you most, and why?*		Can the child explain how the text appealed to them? Is it the illustrations, pictures or information that made that particular pirate interesting?	☐ L5 not attained ☐ Low 5 ☐ Secure 5 ☐ High 5
AF7 Comments identify similarities and differences between texts, with some explanation	Ask: *Can you think of any ways in which this non-fiction book is a bit like a fiction book?*		Can the child make a link between the first-person recounts and the style often used in fictional recounts?	☐ L5 not attained ☐ Low 5 ☐ Secure 5 ☐ High 5

© Oxford University Press: 2010

Copying permitted within purchasing school only

Writing assessment

Ask the child to write a diary entry in role as a sailor who was captured by pirates and made to take the Pirate's Oath and become a member of the crew. Remind them to write in the past tense and first person, and describe what they feel, see and do on their first day as a pirate.

Use the chart below to help you gather information from this piece of writing to assess children's attainment against the Writing Assessment Focuses at Level 5.

Level 5 Assessment Focus guidelines	Notes on child's writing	Ideas for following up child's writing	Best fit NC Level
AF1 Relevant ideas and material developed with some imaginative detail; Development of ideas and material appropriately shaped for selected form; Clear viewpoint established, generally consistent, with some elaboration		Are the ship and other appropriate characters described? Does the diary include details of how the writer feels and what they think? Can we work out if the writer is happy to become a pirate or not? Has the writer played with using pirate language or old-fashioned spellings?	☐ L5 not attained ☐ Low 5 ☐ Secure 5 ☐ High 5
AF2 Main purpose of writing is clear and consistently maintained; Features of selected form clearly established with some adaptation to purpose; Appropriate style clearly established to maintain reader's interest throughout		Is the diary written in chronological order and in the past tense, first person with a personal tone? Is there extra information designed to make the entry more interesting? Does the diary have a sense of tone or voice that draws the reader into its confidence?	☐ L5 not attained ☐ Low 5 ☐ Secure 5 ☐ High 5
AF3 Material is structured clearly, with sentences organised into appropriate paragraphs; Development of material is effectively managed across text; Overall direction of the text supported by clear links between paragraphs		Is there a logical progression through the paragraphs or sections of the diary? Are time connectives used? Does the diary include moments of tension shown by short pacey sentences? Is reported speech used to create a sense of character?	☐ L5 not attained ☐ Low 5 ☐ Secure 5 ☐ High 5
AF4 Paragraphs clearly structure main ideas across the text to support purpose; Within paragraphs/sections, a range of devices support cohesion		Does the child use paragraphs or sections with headings to structure the diary? Is reference made to other parts of the diary, e.g. 'as I said earlier', etc.?	☐ L5 not attained ☐ Low 5 ☐ Secure 5 ☐ High 5
AF5 A variety of sentence lengths, structures and subjects provides clarity and emphasis; Some features of sentence structure used to build up detail or convey shades of meaning		Does the child structure and present their sentences correctly? Do they use connectives to create flow and a variety of verb tenses to show nuances of time? Do their sentences convey emotion, atmosphere and suspense?	☐ L5 not attained ☐ Low 5 ☐ Secure 5 ☐ High 5
AF6 Full range of punctuation used accurately to demarcate sentences, including speech punctuation; Syntax and punctuation within the sentence generally accurate, including commas to mark clauses, although some errors occur where ambitious structures are attempted		Does the child use a range of sentence punctuation correctly? Do they punctuate direct speech accurately? Are commas used in lists and to show subordinate clauses?	☐ L5 not attained ☐ Low 5 ☐ Secure 5 ☐ High 5
AF7 Vocabulary chosen for effect; Reasonably wide vocabulary used, though not always appropriately		Does the child use vocabulary in a way that shows they know the meaning of the words? Do they use interesting words for particular effects? Do they choose vocabulary specific to the pirate theme, including words from their reading?	☐ L5 not attained ☐ Low 5 ☐ Secure 5 ☐ High 5
AF8 Correct spelling of: grammatical function words; almost all inflected words; most derivational suffixes and prefixes; most content/lexical words		Look at any spelling mistakes to assess patterns of error. Are there spelling patterns that need practice?	☐ L5 not attained ☐ Low 5 ☐ Secure 5 ☐ High 5

© Oxford University Press: 2010

Assessment Pointers for Stage 16/National Curriculum Level 4 (based on Stage 16 *Myths and Legends Tales of the Underworld*)

Reading assessment

Use the chart below to help you gather information to assess children's attainment against the Reading Assessment Focuses at Level 4.

Level 4 Assessment Focus guidelines	Suggested prompt	Notes on child's response	Ideas for following up child's response	Best fit NC Level
AF2 Comments supported by some generally relevant textual reference or quotation	When the child has read the story *Orpheus and Eurydice*, ask them to find some evidence that helps to show this story comes from Ancient Greece.		Notice whether the child can refer back to the text and find quotes to back up their suggestions.	☐ L4 not attained ☐ Low 4 ☐ Secure 4 ☐ High 4
AF3 Inferences often correct, but comments are not always rooted securely in the text or repeat narrative or content	After reading *Orpheus and Eurydice*, ask: *Do you think Orpheus deserved this sad ending? Why or why not?*		Prompt the child to give some reasons based on what the author tells us about Orpheus and Eurydice, as well as their personal opinion.	☐ L4 not attained ☐ Low 4 ☐ Secure 4 ☐ High 4
AF4 Some basic features of organisation at text level identified	Ask the child to use the Contents page and the information on the first page of each story to find a story that comes from Australia.		Does the child use the page numbers on the Contents page and scan the first page of each story to find this information?	☐ L4 not attained ☐ Low 4 ☐ Secure 4 ☐ High 4
AF5 Some basic features of writer's use of language identified; Simple comments on writer's choices	Read the first page of *Savitri's Three Wishes* and ask the child what they notice about the length of the sentences the author has used.		Can the child identify that there is a lot of variation in sentence length? Can they make a suggestion about why the author might have decided to vary sentence lengths like this?	☐ L4 not attained ☐ Low 4 ☐ Secure 4 ☐ High 4
AF6 Simple comment on overall effect on reader	Ask the child to say which is their favourite story and explain why.		Can the child explain why they chose this particular story, giving some reasons related to the text and explaining how the story made them feel?	☐ L4 not attained ☐ Low 4 ☐ Secure 4 ☐ High 4
AF7 Features common to different texts identified, with simple comment	Ask the child to pick two of the stories in the book and find things that are similar about the stories, and things that are different.		Can the child identify at least two similarities and differences? Do they look at the author's style as well as the subject matter of the stories?	☐ L4 not attained ☐ Low 4 ☐ Secure 4 ☐ High 4

© Oxford University Press: 2010

Copying permitted within purchasing school only

Writing assessment

Ask the child to choose another myth or traditional story that they know well and to write a retelling of this story. If they wish they could make up a new story in the style of a myth.

Use the chart below to help you gather information from this piece of writing to assess children's attainment against the Writing Assessment Focuses at Level 4.

Level 4 Assessment Focus guidelines	Notes on child's writing	Ideas for following up child's writing	Best fit NC Level
AF1 Relevant ideas and content chosen; Some ideas and material developed in detail		Does the child's story contain details and ideas that are in keeping with the traditional tale/myth genre? Do they expand on some of the ideas, e.g. by describing characters and their motivation in detail?	☐ L4 not attained ☐ Low 4 ☐ Secure 4 ☐ High 4
AF2 Main purpose of writing is clear but not always consistently maintained; Main features of selected form are clear and appropriate to purpose, Style generally appropriate to task, though awareness of reader not always sustained		Does the child maintain an appropriate style for a traditional tale or myth throughout most of the piece?	☐ L4 not attained ☐ Low 4 ☐ Secure 4 ☐ High 4
AF3 Ideas organised: by clustering related points or by time sequence; simply with a fitting opening and closing, sometimes linked; generally in logical sequenced but overall direction of writing not always clearly signalled		Is there a logical progression in the story? Does it follow chronological order, or if it departs from chronological order, is it easy enough for a reader to understand?	☐ L4 not attained ☐ Low 4 ☐ Secure 4 ☐ High 4
AF4 Paragraphs/sections help to organise content; Within paragraphs/sections, limited range of connections between sentences; Some attempts to establish simple links between paragraphs/sections not always maintained		Does the child use paragraphs, or group events under headings that show when they happened? Are there links made between sentences and paragraphs, such as connective phrases?	☐ L4 not attained ☐ Low 4 ☐ Secure 4 ☐ High 4
AF5 Some variety in length, structure or subject of sentences; Some use of subordinating connectives		Does the child include sentences of different lengths and with different structures? Do they use subordinating connectives such as 'when'?	☐ L4 not attained ☐ Low 4 ☐ Secure 4 ☐ High 4
AF6 Sentences demarcated accurately throughout the text, including question marks; Speech marks to denote speech generally accurate, with some other speech punctuation; Commas used in lists and occasionally to mark clauses, although not always accurately		Does the child use a range of final sentence punctuation correctly? Do they attempt to punctuate direct speech? Are commas used in lists and occasionally to show subordinate clauses?	☐ L4 not attained ☐ Low 4 ☐ Secure 4 ☐ High 4
AF7 Some evidence of deliberate vocabulary choices; Some expansion of general vocabulary to match topic		Does the child use vocabulary in a way that shows they know the meaning of the words? Do they sometimes use interesting words for particular effects? Do they use vocabulary appropriate to the traditional tale genre?	☐ L4 not attained ☐ Low 4 ☐ Secure 4 ☐ High 4
AF8 Correct spelling of: most common grammatical function words, including adverbs with '-ly' formation; regularly formed content/ lexical words, including those with multiple morphemes; most past and present tense inflections, plurals		Look at any spelling mistakes to assess patterns of error. Are there spelling patterns that need practice?	☐ L4 not attained ☐ Low 4 ☐ Secure 4 ☐ High 4

Assessment Pointers for Stage 16/National Curriculum Level 5 (based on Stage 16 *Myths and Legends Tales of the Underworld*)

Reading assessment

Use the chart below to help you gather information to assess children's attainment against the Reading Assessment Focuses at Level 5.

Level 5 Assessment Focus guidelines	Suggested prompt	Notes on child's response	Ideas for following up child's response	Best fit NC Level
AF2 Comments generally supported by relevant textual reference or quotation, even when the points made are not always accurate	Choose one of the stories and ask the child to sum up the main meaning or message of the story as briefly as possible. Can they find a quotation from the text that helps to convey the story's message?		Is the child able to summarise the main message of the story without retelling it in detail? Can they find an appropriate quotation from the text?	☐ L5 not attained ☐ Low 5 ☐ Secure 5 ☐ High 5
AF3 Comments develop explanation of inferred meanings drawing on evidence across the text	Choose one of the stories and ask the child to explain how the main character changes from the beginning of the story to the end.		Can the child briefly sum up the main changes the character goes through throughout the story? Can they find some evidence in the story to help them work out how the character is feeling at each point?	☐ L5 not attained ☐ Low 5 ☐ Secure 5 ☐ High 5
AF4 Comments on structural choices show some awareness of author's craft	Looking at *Savitri's Three Wishes*, ask the child why they think the author chose to put chapter breaks where she did. Do they think the chapter breaks are effective?		Can the child identify some reasons for placing chapter breaks where the author did?	☐ L5 not attained ☐ Low 5 ☐ Secure 5 ☐ High 5
AF5 Various features of writer's use of language identified, with some explanation	Read the last three pages of *Orpheus and Eurydice*. Ask: *How does the author make us feel sorry for Orpheus at the end of the story?*		Can the child find some words and phrases that help us to feel sorry for Orpheus?	☐ L5 not attained ☐ Low 5 ☐ Secure 5 ☐ High 5
AF6 General awareness of effect on the reader, with some, often limited, explanation	Ask the child which of the four stories they thought was most moving, and why.		Can the child explain why they thought the chosen story was moving? Can they point to some reasons from the story, over and above their own personal preferences?	☐ L5 not attained ☐ Low 5 ☐ Secure 5 ☐ High 5
AF7 Comments identify similarities and differences between texts, with some explanation	Ask: *How many similarities can you think of between the four stories in this book?*		Does the child refer to the author's style and the way the stories are told, as well as similarities in subject matter?	☐ L5 not attained ☐ Low 5 ☐ Secure 5 ☐ High 5

© Oxford University Press: 2010
Copying permitted within purchasing school only

Writing assessment

Ask the child to choose another myth or traditional story that they know well and to write a retelling of this story. If they wish they could make up a new story in the style of a myth.

Use the chart below to help you gather information from this piece of writing to assess children's attainment against the Writing Assessment Focuses at Level 5.

Level 5 Assessment Focus guidelines	Notes on child's writing	Ideas for following up child's writing	Best fit NC Level
AF1 Relevant ideas and material developed with some imaginative detail; Development of ideas and material appropriately shaped for selected form; Clear viewpoint established, generally consistent, with some elaboration		Does the child develop the story by adding details about the characters' motivation and feelings? Is the viewpoint consistent throughout the story? Are the details appropriate for a traditional tale/myth?	☐ L5 not attained ☐ Low 5 ☐ Secure 5 ☐ High 5
AF2 Main purpose is clear and consistently maintained; Features of selected form clearly established with some adaptation to purpose; Appropriate style clearly established to maintain reader's interest throughout		Is the story written in an appropriate style for a traditional tale/myth? Has the child tried to make the story sound like an oral retelling? Has the child included details and word choices that would make it interesting for a listener/reader?	☐ L5 not attained ☐ Low 5 ☐ Secure 5 ☐ High 5
AF3 Material is structured clearly, with sentences organised into appropriate paragraphs; Development of material is effectively managed across the text; Overall general direction of the text supported by clear links between paragraphs		Is there a logical progression through the paragraphs or sections of the story? Are time connectives used? Is reported speech used to create a sense of character?	☐ L5 not attained ☐ Low 5 ☐ Secure 5 ☐ High 5
AF4 Paragraphs clearly structure main ideas across the text to support purpose; Within paragraphs/sections a range of devices support cohesion		Does the child use paragraphs effectively? Are there links between paragraphs or sections in the story that enable the reader to make connections between earlier and later events?	☐ L5 not attained ☐ Low 5 ☐ Secure 5 ☐ High 5
AF5 A variety of sentence lengths, structures and subjects provides clarity and emphasis; Some features of sentence structure used to build up detail or convey shades of meaning		Does the child structure and present their sentences correctly? Do they use connectives to create flow and a variety of verb tenses to show nuances of time? Do they use a variety of sentence lengths and structures?	☐ L5 not attained ☐ Low 5 ☐ Secure 5 ☐ High 5
AF6 Full range of punctuation used to accurately demarcate sentences, including speech punctuation; Syntax and punctuation within the sentence generally accurate including commas to mark clauses, although some errors occur where ambitious structures are attempted		Does the child use a range of sentence punctuation correctly? Do they punctuate direct speech accurately? Are commas used in lists and to show subordinate clauses?	☐ L5 not attained ☐ Low 5 ☐ Secure 5 ☐ High 5
AF7 Vocabulary chosen for effect; Reasonably wide vocabulary used, though not always appropriately		Does the child use vocabulary in a way that shows they know the meaning of the words? Do they use interesting words for particular effects? Do they choose vocabulary specific to the story theme, including words from their reading?	☐ L5 not attained ☐ Low 5 ☐ Secure 5 ☐ High 5
AF8 Correct spelling of: grammatical function words; almost all inflected words; most derivational suffixes and prefixes; most content/ lexical words		Look at any spelling mistakes to assess patterns of error. Are there spelling patterns that need practice?	☐ L5 not attained ☐ Low 5 ☐ Secure 5 ☐ High 5

Next steps

The charts on pages 64–67 give some ideas for further steps you could take to help children to develop specific reading skills as a follow-up to the assessment process. If you discover that children are struggling with specific skills at a particular National Curriculum Level, you will find suggestions for helping them with these skills in the charts.

Next steps at Level 2

Assessment Focus	Reading behaviour	Suggestions
AF1	Fluency interrupted by frequent need to sound out words, or over-reliance on other strategies	Give the child more reading practice by choosing stories at Stage 9 or Stage 10 to read silently, at home to an adult or aloud in school. In particular, offer lots of encouragement to the child to read aloud, and praise the child when they get a known word right without sounding it out. Target any tricky spelling patterns or difficult words for more practice in class.
AF2	Does not always have a clear grasp of sequence of events	Use the Year 3/P4 TreeTops *Comprehension Pupils' Book* and encourage the child to return to the text and focus on what they have read.
AF3	Finds it hard to make inferences – tends to rely on information that is directly conveyed in the text	While the child is reading, pause from time to time to discuss what is going on in the story and ask them for their opinion. Some children need help to understand that their own opinion on a story is valid – encourage them to express their thoughts and to give reasons related to the text.
AF4	Rereads from the beginning of the book when looking for particular evidence in fiction or non-fiction texts	Use activities from the TreeTops *Teaching Notes*, e.g. for TreeTops *Captain Comet and the Dog Star Fiction* at Stage 9, practise using the Contents page, and for TreeTops *Against All Odds Non-fiction* at Stage 9 revise the use of features of non-fiction texts.
AF5	Finds it hard to identify effective language choices in stories	Use the extract from TreeTops *Captain Comet and the Dog Star* in the Year 3/P4 TreeTops *Comprehension Pupils' Book*. Locate the words and sentences that set the scene for a mystery story. The child could scan the story to find and list words that imply that a character is anxious. They could also find short sentences that create tension, e.g. 'But there was no reply.'
AF6	Enjoys stories but finds it hard to articulate a personal response other than 'I liked it'	Ask the child to talk about their favourite character and/or their favourite incident in a book. Encourage them to explain why they liked a character or event in the story.
AF7	Needs help in considering a story in context	Talk with the child about other books or comics they may have read, or TV programmes and films they have seen, that are in a similar genre to a TreeTops book. For example, for TreeTops *Captain Comet and the Dog Star*, they may have read other science fiction stories or comics, or seen a science fiction film. Encourage them to think of similarities and differences, and to express their opinions about which they enjoyed most and why.

Next steps at Level 3

Assessment Focus	Reading behaviour	Suggestions
AF1	Reading is competent but with little or no expression, implying poor understanding of the text	Show the child how to scan ahead to the end of the sentence to notice question or exclamation marks. Note the way this changes expression. Practise reading with expression TreeTops *Playscripts* at Stages 12 and 13, using the stage directions to prompt the appropriate style of reading.
AF2	Struggles to find evidence in the text to answer questions or support statements	Use the Year 4/P5 TreeTops *Comprehension* components to give the child practice in identifying evidence from texts and picking out details to answer questions.
AF3	Can describe events as explained in text but finds it hard to empathise with characters and their feelings	You could use role play activities such as hotseating to encourage the child to empathise with the characters in a story, e.g. using TreeTops *The Lie Detector Playscripts* at Stage 12, hotseat Laura after Scene 3 and again at the end of the play.
AF4	Struggles to explain the differences between fiction and non-fiction texts	Ask the child to focus on just one page or one spread from a fiction book, a non-fiction book and a playscript. You could ask children to work in pairs and make a list of all the relevant text type features they can find in each case. Then pool lists to make a whole-class master list. If the children struggle to remember the differences between the text types, encourage them to make a poster for display on the wall, with as many of the different text type features shown as possible.
AF5	Can talk about the text but now needs to develop an awareness of the writer's vocabulary and style	For example, working with TreeTops *The Lie Detector Playscripts* explain that this play is written in a very natural style so that it really sounds like people talking. Compare the playscript with a range of other books, e.g. including a more formal novel, a non-fiction text and a picture book with little dialogue. Encourage the child to make comparisons and point out differences. Ask them to find some good examples of dialogue that sound very realistic.
AF6	Enjoys reading, but finds it hard to articulate a personal response	Ask the child to show you the parts of a book or playscript that they enjoyed the most. Encourage them to discuss these parts with a partner and share their thoughts about different parts of the text in a group. Encourage everyone to take turns to say what they liked and why, and to listen to others.
AF7	Needs help in making links between texts	Give the child a few books by the same author, or books in the same genre. Ask them to look for things that are similar across the books, e.g. similar themes, a similar style, etc. You may need to model this for them the first time, so they can see the types of connections that you are making.

Next steps at Level 4

Assessment Focus	Reading behaviour	Suggestions
AF1	Fluency interrupted by unfamiliar vocabulary or unusual words	Support the breaking down of unfamiliar words or words from the past by modelling how to read them and discussing their meanings before you begin reading. Treetops *Myths and Legends* books contain pronunciation guides to help with more difficult words, it may help to model the use of these guides before you begin reading. Any tricky spelling patterns or difficult words can be targeted for more practice in class.
AF2	Reads fluently but may not always pick up relevant information from the text	Encourage the child to build up a mental picture of the text that they read, and keep on adding details to their mental picture as they progress through the text. Stop occasionally to discuss the text and share questions and thoughts about it. Some children may like to keep notes or draw sketches to remind them of the main points of the story as they read.
AF3	Finds it hard to understand characters' motives	When working with, for example, TreeTops *The Secret Garden Classics* at Stage 14 use the *Teaching Notes* to explore Mary's character. Encourage the child to form their own opinion of her, built up from all the clues in the text. Ask the child to compare her life in India with her life at Misselthwaite. Does this help to explain how she behaves at Misselthwaite?
AF4	Finds it hard to explain how the text is organised for impact or interest	Look together at the beginning and ending of each chapter in a book the child is reading. Can the child identify the way chapters end, e.g. at an exciting point or cliffhanger, or at the end of a piece of action?
AF5	Can talk about the events and characters but now needs to develop an awareness of the writer's vocabulary and style	Look at how the author uses description in a story, and ask the child to pick out one or two effective examples of description. Can they write their own short descriptions of a setting in a similar style?
AF6	Enjoys stories but finds it hard to articulate how the writer has created an effect, for example, made a tense atmosphere	When working with the TreeTops *The Secret Garden*, discuss the 'secret' aspect of the story and ask the child to think about how the author returns to the theme of secrets throughout the book. Ask the child to decide which secret caused the most tension in the book – Colin hidden away, the garden hidden away or Mary keeping the garden secret once she had discovered it?
AF7	Needs help in considering a story in context	Ask the child what they knew about Victorian Britain (if anything) before they read the TreeTops *The Secret Garden*. Can they identify some things they found out about life at that time from reading the book? Try the same activity with other books set in the past, or with books set in different locations, e.g. *Climbing in the Dark Fiction* at Stage 14. Try comparing information found in stories set at a similar time or in similar locations.

Next steps at Level 5

Assessment Focus	Reading behaviour	Suggestions
AF1	Fluency interrupted by unfamiliar vocabulary or unusual words	Support the breaking down of unfamiliar words, or words derived from the past or from other cultures, by looking at the cultural/geographical roots of words and talking about their meanings. Treetops *Myths and Legends* books contain pronunciation guides to help with more difficult words, it may help to model the use of these guides before you begin reading. Any tricky spelling patterns or difficult words can be targeted for more practice in class.
AF2	Selects and retrieves information from the text but sometimes has difficulty explaining what the information means in context	Use the Year 6/P7 TreeTops *Comprehension Pupils' Books* to practise summarising and explaining the key points of texts and expressing these in their own words.
AF3	Can understand that the text explores different ideas about a topic, but finds it hard to draw the ideas together from across the text	When working with TreeTops *Pirates Non-fiction* at Stage 15 use the *Teaching Notes* to explore how to use mind-mapping to bring key ideas together in one place. Ask the child to practise collecting key ideas from across the whole text under headings such as 'What is piracy?', 'Who were pirates?', 'How did you become a pirate?'
AF4	Can use the text to find information but finds it hard to explain how the text is organised for impact or interest	Ask the child to select a favourite part of a non-fiction book and explain to a partner why they like it. Prompt them to focus on how the text is organised – for example, is it easy to find information? Is it designed in an eye-catching way? Are the illustrations appropriate? Do the headings help to structure the text clearly?
AF5	Can talk about the key ideas but now needs to develop an awareness of the writer's vocabulary and style	Together, look at the introduction of a non-fiction book, or the first chapter of a novel, and invite the child to say whether it makes them want to read on. What aspects of the introduction or first chapter make them want to read the rest of the book? Do they think the author has done a good job of stirring up the reader's interest?
AF6	Enjoys the text but finds it hard to explain why they enjoy it	In pairs, ask the children to choose their favourite part of a non-fiction text and explain why they like it. You could organise it as a class competition, so that children get one point for each sensible reason they can think of to explain why the text is effective. The child with the most points wins!
AF7	Needs help in considering the information in context	When working with TreeTops *Pirates*, encourage the child to think about how our modern perceptions of pirates as having an exciting and romantic life are not based on historical evidence. Can the child use the text to find three reasons why being a pirate might be an unpleasant experience?

Skills checklists

The checklists on the following pages list the main reading skills which children will usually be developing while they use TreeTops resources at each Stage.

For each TreeTops Stage, you will find a checklist of skills for teacher's use and a self-assessment sheet that covers the same skills using child-friendly language.

You can use the teacher's checklists for a quick assessment check, either with an individual child or with a reading group. On the teacher's checklists you will find cross-references to both the Primary National Strategy Literacy Framework Objectives and the Assessment Focuses, for ease of record-keeping and planning.

Children can fill in their own self-assessment sheets to record their progress and attitude towards reading. They can make marks in the relevant boxes, with a 'thumbs up' for skills they find easy to do, a neutral symbol for skills that they can do most of the time and a 'thumbs down' for skills that they find difficult.

You may find it most effective to use the sheets towards the end of the relevant TreeTops Stage, but they can also be used for a quick check while children are working through the Stage, to help you identify areas where practice or support are needed. The same skills are featured across more than one TreeTops Stage, and it is to be expected that children may not achieve all of the skills at every Stage.

Stage 16   **Self-assessment sheet**

Name: Sarah Matthews   Date: 24th October

| | I can do this well. | | I can do this most of the time. | | I find this difficult. |

Assessment Focuses	Reading skills	👍	✋	👎
AF2, 6	I can read an information text and quickly make a judgement about the quality of its content and how useful it would be to me.	✓		
AF3	I can talk about the themes and main ideas in texts and identify how the author puts these across.	✓		
AF4	I can explain why authors use connective language, group ideas into paragraphs and use organisational features such as sub-headings.	✓		
AF1, 3	I can explore how words change their meaning when used in different contexts.		✓	
AF3, 5	I can identify when an author uses language to cause an emotional response in the reader and detect the author's point of view or even bias.		✓	
AF6	I can share my opinion about the books I have read, giving examples from the text to back up my judgement.	✓		
AF2, 3, 7	I can keep a reading journal with different types of responses, story-mapping, writing in role, predictions, annotated pictures, etc.	✓		
AF7	I can compare how writers from different times and places present experiences and use language.		✓	

Books I have enjoyed reading: The Secret Garden, Luke Lively and The Castle of Sleep, Freedom Train

I would like more help with looking at how the author uses language and why they choose to use certain words

Signed Sarah Matthews

84   © Oxford University Press: 2010   Copying permitted within purchasing school only

Stage 9 checklist of reading skills

Numbers in brackets refer to the Primary National Strategy Literacy Framework Objectives, e.g. **(8.2)** means strand 8, bullet point 2.

Group .... Date ....

Name ....

Assessment Focuses	Year 2 Reading skills	Comments
AF1	Use phonological, contextual, grammatical and graphic knowledge to work out, predict and check the meanings of unfamiliar words and to make sense of what they read **(Strand 5)**	
AF1	Read independently and with increasing fluency longer and less familiar texts **(5.1)**	
AF2	Draw together ideas and information from across a whole text, using simple signposts in the text **(7.1)**	
AF3	Give some reasons why things happen or characters change **(7.2)**	
AF4	Explain organisational features of texts, including alphabetical order, layout, diagrams, captions, hyperlinks and bullet points **(7.3)**	
AF1	Use syntax and context to build their store of vocabulary when reading for meaning **(7.4)**	
AF5	Explore how particular words are used, including words and expressions with similar meanings **(7.5)**	
AF6	Read whole books on their own, choosing and justifying selections **(8.1)**	
AF3	Engage with books through exploring and enacting interpretations **(8.2)**	
AF6	Explain their reactions to texts, commenting on important aspects **(8.3)**	

Stage 9 covers the reading skills used in Years 2 and 3. For Year 3 reading skills, see the Stage 10 checklist of reading skills on page 71.

Name .... Date ....

	I can do this well.		I can do this most of the time.		I find this difficult.

Assessment Focuses	Reading skills	👍	✋	👎
AF1	I can work out how to read new words by blending sounds.			
AF1	I can read whole books on my own, without help, and read aloud to an audience with expression.			
AF2	I can discuss facts and events I have read about and find the place in the book.			
AF3	I can explain why certain things happened in the story and suggest how characters were feeling.			
AF4	I can explain why the author has used some kinds of punctuation, e.g. words in capital letters, exclamation marks, bullet points.			
AF1	I can work out what new words mean by using the sense of the sentence and what I have already read.			
AF5	I can talk about the words the author has chosen and why they are effective.			
AF6	I can choose a book myself and say what it is about and what I like or do not like about it.			
AF3	I can work in a group to act out a story we have read or explain information to the class.			
AF6	I can talk about other books that this book reminds me of and say why they are similar.			

What I like about reading is ....

....

I would like more help with ....

....

Signed ....

© Oxford University Press: 2010   Copying permitted within purchasing school only

Stage 10 checklist of reading skills

Numbers in brackets refer to the Primary National Strategy Literacy Framework Objectives, e.g. (**8.2**) means strand 8, bullet point 2.

Group .... Date ....

Name ....

Assessment Focuses	Year 3 Reading skills	Comments
AF1	Use phonological, contextual, grammatical and graphic knowledge to work out, predict and check the meanings of unfamiliar words and to make sense of what they read (**Strand 5**)	
AF1	Read independently and with increasing fluency longer and less familiar texts (**Y2 5.1**)	
AF2	Identify and make notes of the main points of section(s) of text (**7.1**)	
AF3	Infer characters' feelings in fiction and consequences in logical explanations (**7.2**)	
AF4	Identify how different texts are organised, including reference texts, magazines and leaflets on paper and on screen (**7.3**)	
AF1	Use syntax, context and word structure to build their store of vocabulary as they read for meaning (**7.4**)	
AF5	Explore how different texts appeal to readers using varied sentence structures and descriptive language (**7.5**)	
AF6	Share and compare reasons for reading preferences, extending the range of books read (**8.1**)	
AF3	Empathise with characters and debate moral dilemmas portrayed in texts (**8.2**)	
AF6	Identify features that writers use to provoke readers' reactions (**8.3**)	

© Oxford University Press: 2010 Copying permitted within purchasing school only

Stage 10 — Self-assessment sheet

Name .... Date ....

	I can do this well.		I can do this most of the time.		I find this difficult.

Assessment Focuses	Reading skills	👍	✋	👎
AF1	I can work out how to read new words by blending sounds.			
AF1	I can read books on my own, without help, and use punctuation to read aloud to an audience with expression.			
AF2	I can talk about the main points in a book and find the information on the page.			
AF3	I can say why characters behaved as they did and talk about their feelings.			
AF4	I can talk about using a contents list and index, and explain how headings and captions help us find information.			
AF1	I can work out what new words mean by using the sense of the sentence, illustrations and diagrams.			
AF5	I can notice how the writer varies sentences and uses particular words to keep the reader's interest.			
AF6	I can talk to others about books and compare our likes and dislikes.			
AF3	I can discuss what happened in the book and say whether I would have done the same thing and why.			
AF6	I can talk about the way a writer makes a story exciting or information interesting.			

What I like about reading is ....

....

I would like more help with ....

....

....

Signed ....

© Oxford University Press: 2010   Copying permitted within purchasing school only

Stage 11 checklist of reading skills

Numbers in brackets refer to the Primary National Strategy Literacy Framework Objectives, e.g. (**8.2**) means strand 8, bullet point 2.

Group .... Date ....

Name ....

Assessment Focuses	Year 3 Reading skills	Comments
AF1	Use phonological, contextual, grammatical and graphic knowledge to work out, predict and check the meanings of unfamiliar words and to make sense of what they read (**Strand 5**)	
AF1	Read independently and with increasing fluency longer and less familiar texts (**Y2 5.1**)	
AF2	Identify and make notes of the main points of section(s) of text (**7.1**)	
AF3	Infer characters' feelings in fiction and consequences in logical explanations (**7.2**)	
AF4	Identify how different texts are organised, including reference texts, magazines and leaflets on paper and on screen (**7.3**)	
AF1	Use syntax, context and word structure to build their store of vocabulary as they read for meaning (**7.4**)	
AF5	Explore how different texts appeal to readers using varied sentence structures and descriptive language (**7.5**)	
AF6	Share and compare reasons for reading preferences, extending the range of books read (**8.1**)	
AF3	Empathise with characters and debate moral dilemmas portrayed in texts (**8.2**)	
AF6	Identify features that writers use to provoke readers' reactions (**8.3**)	

Self-assessment sheet

Name .... Date ....

	I can do this well.		I can do this most of the time.		I find this difficult.

Assessment Focuses	Reading skills	👍	✋	👎
AF1	I can work out how to read new words by blending sounds.			
AF1	I can read books on my own, without help, and use punctuation to read aloud to an audience with expression.			
AF2	I can support my answers and ideas about a book by finding quotations in the text.			
AF3	I can refer to characters' actions and say why they behaved as they did.			
AF4	I can explain why the author sets things out in a certain way or tells a story in a particular order.			
AF1	I can work out what new words mean by using the sense of the sentence, illustrations and diagrams.			
AF5	I can explain how the author uses certain sentences and words to keep the readers' attention.			
AF6	I can read all kinds of books and talk to others about why we like or dislike them.			
AF3	I can talk about dilemmas in a story and explain both sides of the argument.			
AF6	I can talk about the way a writer involves the reader in the story or information.			

What I like about reading is ....

....

I would like more help with ....

....

Signed ....

© Oxford University Press: 2010   Copying permitted within purchasing school only

Stage 12 checklist of reading skills

Numbers in brackets refer to the Primary National Strategy Literacy Framework Objectives, e.g. (**8.2**) means strand 8, bullet point 2.

Group .... Date ....

Name ....

Assessment Focuses	Year 4 Reading skills	Comments
AF2	Identify and summarise evidence from a text to support a hypothesis (**7.1**)	
AF3	Deduce characters' reasons for behaviour from their actions and explain how ideas are developed in non-fiction texts (**7.2**)	
AF4	Use knowledge of different organisational features of texts to find information effectively (**7.3**)	
AF1	Use knowledge of word structures and origins to develop their understanding of word meanings (**7.4**)	
AF5	Explain how writers use figurative and expressive language to create images and atmosphere (**7.5**)	
AF7	Read extensively favourite authors or genres and experiment with other types of text (**8.1**)	
AF2, 3, 6	Interrogate texts to deepen and clarify understanding and response (**8.2**)	
AF6	Explore why and how writers write, including through face-to-face and online contact with authors (**8.3**)	

Self-assessment sheet

Name .... Date ....

	I can do this well.		I can do this most of the time.		I find this difficult.

Assessment Focuses	Reading skills			
AF2	I can find the words and information in the text that support my opinions about a book.			
AF3	I can work out what characters are thinking from what they do and say.			
AF4	I can find the logical sequence of ideas in non-fiction books.			
AF4	I can use headings, captions, a contents list and the index to find information quickly.			
AF1	I can work out what words mean by breaking down a long word into shorter parts and noticing links with other words (e.g. 'comparatively': 'compare').			
AF5	I can talk about a writer's style of writing and say how they create suspense or humour.			
AF7	I can read many books and say why certain authors or kinds of books are my favourites.			
AF2, 3, 6	I can see how one book has similar ideas or settings to another and can make comments on shared themes and ideas.			
AF6	I can contact writers on websites or in visits and talk to them about how they write.			

Books I have enjoyed reading: ....

....

....

I would like more help with ....

....

....

Signed ....

© Oxford University Press: 2010   Copying permitted within purchasing school only

Stage 13 checklist of reading skills

Numbers in brackets refer to the Primary National Strategy Literacy Framework Objectives, e.g. (**8.2**) means strand 8, bullet point 2.

Group .... Date ....

Name ....

Assessment Focuses	Year 5 Reading skills	Comments
AF2, 3	Make notes on and use evidence from across a text to explain events or ideas (**7.1**)	
AF6	Infer writers' perspectives from what is written and from what is implied (**7.2**)	
AF4	Compare different types of narrative and information texts and identify how they are structured (**7.3**)	
AF1, 3	Distinguish between everyday use of words and their subject-specific use (**7.4**)	
AF5	Explore how writers use language for comic and dramatic effects (**7.5**)	
AF6, 7	Reflect on reading habits and preferences and plan personal reading goals (**8.1**)	
AF3	Compare the usefulness of techniques such as visualisation, prediction and empathy in exploring the meaning of texts (**8.2**)	
AF7	Compare how a common theme is presented in poetry, prose and other media (**8.3**)	

Stage 13 covers the reading skills used in Years 4 and 5. For Year 4 reading skills, see the Stage 12 checklist of reading skills chart on page 75.

Self-assessment sheet

Name .... Date ....

👍	I can do this well.	✋	I can do this most of the time.	👎	I find this difficult.

Assessment Focuses	Reading skills	👍	✋	👎
AF2, 3	I can make notes about a text and then use evidence in the text to explain events or ideas.			
AF6	I can make inferences about the writers' points of view from what is written and from what is suggested.			
AF4	I can compare different types of information texts and fiction texts and identify how they are structured.			
AF1, 3	I can understand that some words have an everyday use as well as a use within a particular subject (for example 'result' used in a science experiment and to describe a final score in a match).			
AF5	I can explore how writers use language to create humour and tension.			
AF6, 7	I can think about the reasons why I choose to read certain stories or texts and use this to plan what I will read in the future.			
AF3	I can use a variety of techniques such as visualisation, prediction and empathy in exploring the meaning of texts and decide which techniques work best for me.			
AF7	I can read a poem, story or play and watch a film or video clip and comment on how they explore the same subject or theme.			

Books I have enjoyed reading: ....

....

I would like more help with ....

....

....

Signed ....

© Oxford University Press: 2010   Copying permitted within purchasing school only

Stage 14 checklist of reading skills

Numbers in brackets refer to the Primary National Strategy Literacy Framework Objectives, e.g. (**8.2**) means strand 8, bullet point 2.

Group .... Date ....

Name ....

Assessment Focuses	Year 5 Reading skills	Comments
AF2, 3	Make notes on and use evidence from across a text to explain events or ideas (**7.1**)	
AF6	Infer writers' perspectives from what is written and from what is implied (**7.2**)	
AF4	Compare different types of narrative and information texts and identify how they are structured (**7.3**)	
AF1, 3	Distinguish between everyday use of words and their subject-specific use (**7.4**)	
AF5	Explore how writers use language for comic and dramatic effects (**7.5**)	
AF6, 7	Reflect on reading habits and preferences and plan personal reading goals (**8.1**)	
AF3	Compare the usefulness of techniques such as visualisation, prediction and empathy in exploring the meaning of texts (**8.2**)	
AF7	Compare how a common theme is presented in poetry, prose and other media (**8.3**)	

Self-assessment sheet

Name .... Date ....

| | | I can do this well. | | I can do this most of the time. | | I find this difficult. |

Assessment Focuses	Reading skills	👍	✋	👎
AF2, 3	I can make notes about a text and then use evidence in the text to explain events or ideas.			
AF6	I can make inferences about the writers' points of view from what is written and from what is suggested.			
AF4	I can compare different types of information texts and fiction texts and identify how they are structured.			
AF1, 3	I can understand that some words have an everyday use as well as a use within a particular subject (for example 'result' used in a science experiment and to describe a final score in a match).			
AF5	I can explore how writers use language to create humour and tension.			
AF6, 7	I can think about the reasons why I choose to read certain stories or texts and use this to plan what I will read in the future.			
AF3	I can use a variety of techniques such as visualisation, prediction and empathy in exploring the meaning of texts and decide which techniques work best for me.			
AF7	I can read a poem, story or play and watch a film or video clip and comment on how they explore the same subject or theme.			

Books I have enjoyed reading: ....

....

....

I would like more help with ....

....

....

Signed ....

© Oxford University Press: 2010   Copying permitted within purchasing school only

Stage 15 checklist of reading skills

Numbers in brackets refer to the Primary National Strategy Literacy Framework Objectives, e.g. **(8.2)** means strand 8, bullet point 2.

Group .... Date ....

Name ....

Assessment Focuses	Year 6 Reading skills	Comments
AF2, 6	Appraise a text quickly, deciding on its value, quality or usefulness **(7.1)**	
AF2, 3	Understand underlying themes, causes and points of view **(7.2)**	
AF4	Understand how writers use different structures to create coherence and impact **(7.3)**	
AF1, 3	Explore how word meanings change when used in different contexts **(7.4)**	
AF3, 5	Recognise rhetorical devices used to argue, persuade, mislead and sway the reader **(7.5)**	
AF6	Read extensively and discuss personal reading with others, including in reading groups **(8.1)**	
AF2, 3, 6	Sustain engagement with longer texts, using different techniques to make the text come alive **(8.2)** (e.g. visualisation, reading journal entries, further research about the main themes or topic of the book)	
AF7	Compare how writers from different times and places present experiences and use language **(8.3)**	

Self-assessment sheet

Name .... Date ....

		I can do this well.		I can do this most of the time.		I find this difficult.

Assessment Focuses	Reading skills			
AF2, 6	I can read an information text and quickly make a judgement about the quality of its content and how useful it would be to me.			
AF2, 3	I can talk about the themes and main ideas in texts and identify how the author puts these across.			
AF4	I can explain why authors use connective language, group ideas into paragraphs and use organisational features such as sub-headings.			
AF1, 3	I can explore how words change their meaning when used in different contexts.			
AF3, 5	I can identify when an author uses language to cause an emotional response in the reader and detect the author's point of view or even bias.			
AF6	I can share my opinion about the books I have read, giving examples from the text to back up my judgement.			
AF2, 3, 6	I can keep a reading journal with different types of responses, story-mapping, writing in role, predictions, annotated pictures, etc.			
AF7	I can compare how writers from different times and places present experiences and use language.			

Books I have enjoyed reading: ....

....

I would like more help with ....

....

....

Signed ....

 © Oxford University Press: 2010   Copying permitted within purchasing school only

Stage 16 checklist of reading skills

Numbers in brackets refer to the Primary National Strategy Literacy Framework Objectives, e.g. (**8.2**) means strand 8, bullet point 2.

Group .... Date ....

Name ....

Assessment Focuses	Year 6 Reading skills	Comments
AF2, 6	Appraise a text quickly, deciding on its value, quality or usefulness (**7.1**)	
AF2, 3	Understand underlying themes, causes and points of view (**7.2**)	
AF4	Understand how writers use different structures to create coherence and impact (**7.3**)	
AF1, 3	Explore how word meanings change when used in different contexts (**7.4**)	
AF3, 5	Recognise rhetorical devices used to argue, persuade, mislead and sway the reader (**7.5**)	
AF6	Read extensively and discuss personal reading with others, including in reading groups (**8.1**)	
AF2, 3, 7	Sustain engagement with longer texts, using different techniques to make the text come alive (**8.2**) (e.g. visualisation, reading journal entries, further research about the main themes or topic of the book)	
AF7	Compare how writers from different times and places present experiences and use language (**8.3**)	

Self-assessment sheet

Name .... Date ....

| | | 👍 I can do this well. | ✋ I can do this most of the time. | 👎 I find this difficult. |

Assessment Focuses	Reading skills	👍	✋	👎
AF2, 6	I can read an information text and quickly make a judgement about the quality of its content and how useful it would be to me.			
AF2, 3	I can talk about the themes and main ideas in texts and identify how the author puts these across.			
AF4	I can explain why authors use connective language, group ideas into paragraphs and use organisational features such as sub-headings.			
AF1, 3	I can explore how words change their meaning when used in different contexts.			
AF3, 5	I can identify when an author uses language to cause an emotional response in the reader and detect the author's point of view or even bias.			
AF6	I can share my opinion about the books I have read, giving examples from the text to back up my judgement.			
AF2, 3, 7	I can keep a reading journal with different types of responses, story-mapping, writing in role, predictions, annotated pictures, etc.			
AF7	I can compare how writers from different times and places present experiences and use language.			

Books I have enjoyed reading: ....

....

I would like more help with ....

....

....

Signed ....

© Oxford University Press: 2010   Copying permitted within purchasing school only

Fiction overview (including Book Bands and Curriculum Levels)

The chart that follows shows the Key Stage 2 Book Band and National Curriculum Levels for each Stage of TreeTops fiction, plus curriculum correlation information for Northern Ireland and Wales. It also shows the genre of each fiction title, to help you select the most appropriate stories for your children's needs.

Book Band Curriculum Level in England, Wales and Northern Ireland	Stories with familiar settings	Traditional stories, myths and legends	Adventure and mystery	Historical setting	Fantasy, imaginary worlds and science fiction	Different cultures (contemporary/ non-traditional stories)
Stage 9 **Key Stage 2 Book Band:** Year 3, Brown **Best fit National Curriculum in England Level:** 2 **National Curriculum for Wales Level:** 2 **Northern Ireland Curriculum Level:** 2	**Fiction** *Noisy Neighbours* *Robo-Vac* *The Big Little Dinosaur* **Fiction More Stories A** *The Cowboy Next Door* *Oh, Otto!*	**Fiction** *Messy Ella* (retelling of Cinderella) **Myths and Legends** *Wolf Fables* *Floods* *The Legend of Robin Hood*	**Fiction** *The Spooks*		**Fiction** *Captain Comet and the Purple Planet* **Fiction** **More Stories A** *Bigboots the Spider* *Princess Pip's Holiday* *Captain Comet and the Dog Star* *Walrus Joins In*	
Stage 10 **Key Stage 2 Book Band:** Year 3, Brown **Best fit National Curriculum in England Level:** 2 **National Curriculum for Wales Level:** 2 **Northern Ireland Curriculum Level:** 2	**Fiction** *The Boss Dog of Blossom Street* *The Squink* *Jungle Shorts* **Fiction More Stories A** *The Great Spaghetti Suit* *Stupid Trousers* *Jellyfish Shoes* *Purple Buttons* **Fiction More Stories B** *Cornflake Coin* *Micro the Metal Dog* *Dustbin* **Playscripts** *Stupid Trousers*	**Myths and Legends** *Animal Tricksters* *Gods of Thunder* *Merlin and the Lost King of England*	**Fiction** *Mr Stofflees and the Painted Tiger* **Fiction More Stories A** *Dexter's Dinosaurs* **Fiction More Stories B** *The Ghost Ship* *Half Price Hero*		**Fiction** *The Masked Cleaning Ladies of Om* *The Masked Cleaning Ladies Save the Day* **Fiction** **More Stories A** *The Masked Cleaning Ladies Meet the Pirates* **Fiction** **More Stories B** *Fast Frog* **Playscripts** *The Masked Cleaning Ladies of Om*	

Book Band Curriculum Level in England, Wales and Northern Ireland	Stories with familiar settings	Traditional stories, myths and legends	Adventure and mystery	Historical setting	Fantasy, imaginary worlds and science fiction	Different cultures (contemporary/non-traditional stories)
Key Stage 2 Book Band: Year 3, Brown **Best fit National Curriculum in England Level: 2/3** **National Curriculum for Wales Level: 2/3** **Northern Ireland Curriculum Level: 2/3** Stage 11	**Fiction** *Amy the Hedgehog Girl* *Coming Clean* *Hard to Please* *Flans Across the River* *Bertie Wiggins' Amazing Ears* *Bertha's Secret Battle* **Fiction More Stories A** *The Big Chance* *An Odd Job for Bob and Benny* *Janey's Giants* *The Wrong Letter* **Fiction More Stories B** *Stinky Street* *My Dad Does Belly Dancing* *Robot Childminder* **Playscripts** *Bertha's Secret Battle* *Bertie Wiggins' Amazing Ears*	**Fiction More Stories B** *The Fabulous Food Machine* (version of *The Emperor's New Clothes*) **Myths and Legends** *Fables from Africa* *When a Cat Ruled the World* *Hercules the Hero*	**Fiction More Stories A** *Blackbones Saves the School* *Dangerous Trainers*		**Fiction More Stories B** *Jem Stone Genie and the Crash* *The Luckless Monster*	

© Oxford University Press: 2010

Copying permitted within purchasing school only

Book Band Curriculum Level in England, Wales and Northern Ireland	Stories with familiar settings	Traditional stories, myths and legends	Adventure and mystery	Historical setting	Fantasy, imaginary worlds and science fiction	Different cultures (contemporary/ non-traditional stories)
Key Stage 2 Book Band: Year 4, Grey **Best fit National Curriculum in England Level:** 3/4 **National Curriculum for Wales Level:** 3/4 **Northern Ireland Curriculum Level:** 3/4	**Fiction** *Cool Clive* *Clive Keeps his Cool* *Hamper's Great Escape* *The Lie Detector* **Fiction More Stories A** *Here Comes Trouble* *Snooty Prune* *Pass the Ball!* *Shelly Holmes Ace Detective* *Cool Clive and the Little Pest* *Billy's Luck* **Fiction More Stories B** *Dads Win Prizes* *Me and my Newt* **Fiction More Stories C** *Shelly Holmes Animal Trainer* *Doughnut Dilemma* *Cool Clive and the Bubble Trouble* **Playscripts** *The Lie Detector* *Blue Shoes*	**Fiction** *Robbie Woods and his Merry Men* **Myths and Legends** *King Midas and other tales* *How the World Began* *Rama's Journey*	**Fiction More Stories B** *Kid Wonder and the Terrible Truth* **Fiction More Stories C** *Kid Wonder and the Half-Hearted Hero* *Kid Wonder and the Sticky Skyscraper*	**Fiction More Stories B** *A Kitten in Daisy Street* (Victorian)	**Fiction** *Scrapman* **Fiction** **More Stories B** *Scrapman and Scrapcat* *Doohickey and the Robot* **Fiction** **More Stories C** *Scrapman and the Incredible Flying Machine*	

© Oxford University Press: 2010

Book Band / Curriculum Level in England, Wales and Northern Ireland	Stories with familiar settings	Traditional stories, myths and legends	Adventure and mystery	Historical setting	Fantasy, imaginary worlds and science fiction	Different cultures (contemporary/non-traditional stories)
Stage 13 — **Key Stage 2 Book Band:** Year 4, Grey; Year 5, Blue **Best fit National Curriculum in England Level: 3/4** **National Curriculum for Wales Level: 3/4** **Northern Ireland Curriculum Level: 3/4**	**Fiction** *Waiting for Goldie* *The Goalie's Secret* **Fiction More Stories B** *Pet Squad* *The True Diary of Carly Ann Potter* *Cat Out of the Bag*	**Myths and Legends** *How Winter Came into the World* *Why the Sea is Salty* *Helen of Troy*	**Fiction** *I Wish, I Wish* *The Case of the Smiling Shark* *The Personality Potion* *The Ultimate Trainers* **Fiction More Stories A** *Black Dan* *Bones* *Spooky!* *The Goalie from Nowhere* *The Monster in the Wardrobe* *The Revenge of Captain Blood* **Fiction More Stories B** *Star Struck* *The Anti-Bully Machine* **Playscripts** *Spooky!* *The Personality Potion*	**Graphic Novels** *Cave of Secrets* (prehistoric times) *Hollywood Here I Come* (1920s) *Raiders of the Seas* (18th Century pirates) *The First Emperor* (Chinese history) *The Golden Scarab* (Ancient Egypt)	**Fiction** **More Stories B** *The Quest for the Golden See-saw*	**Graphic Novels** *Chimpanzee Chum* (set in Africa)
Stage 14 — **Key Stage 2 Book Band:** Year 5, Blue **Best fit National Curriculum in England Level: 3/4** **National Curriculum for Wales Level: 3/4** **Northern Ireland Curriculum Level: 3/4**	**Fiction** *Danny's Secret Fox* *Okay, Spanner, You Win!* **Fiction More Stories A** *The Booming Boots of Joey Jones*	**Myths and Legends** *Dragon Tales* *The Star Fruit Tree and other stories* *Beowulf, Grendel and the Dragon*	**Fiction More Stories A** *Trapped!* *The Terrible Power of House Rabbit* *Never Wash your Hair* **Classics** *The Jungle Book* *The Three Musketeers* *White Fang* *The Canterville Ghost*	**Fiction** *Climbing in the Dark* (Victorian) *Grace the Pirate* (18th Century) **Fiction More Stories A** *Sing for your Supper* (18th Century) *Air Raid!* (Second World War) **Classics** *The Secret Garden* (Victorian) *Five Children and It* (Victorian/Edwardian) **Graphic Novels** *Cocoa Warriors* (16th Century) *Fire Mountain* (Roman) *In a Class of her Own* (1960s) *Marco Polo and the Roc* (13th Century) *Nellie in the News* (19th Century) *The Taj* (Indian history) **Playscripts** *Climbing in the Dark*	**Fiction** *Petey* *The Night of the Ticklers* **Playscripts** *Petey*	

© Oxford University Press: 2010   Copying permitted within purchasing school only

Book Band Curriculum Level in England, Wales and Northern Ireland	Stories with familiar settings	Traditional stories, myths and legends	Adventure and mystery	Historical setting	Fantasy, imaginary worlds and science fiction	Different cultures (contemporary/ non-traditional stories)
Key Stage 2 Book Band: Year 6, Red **Best fit National Curriculum in England Level: 4/5** **National Curriculum for Wales Level: 4/5** **Northern Ireland Curriculum Level: 4/5**	**Fiction** *The Worst Team in the World* *Soccer Showdowns* **Fiction More Stories A** *My Guinea-Pig is Innocent*	**Myths and Legends** *Mythical Beasts and Fabulous Monsters* *Why Dogs Have Black Noses* *The Journey of Odysseus*	**Fiction** *The Ghosts of Bracken Hill* *A Spell of Trouble* **Fiction More Stories A** *The Mean Dream Wonder Machine* *Go to the Dragon-maker* **Classics** *Moonfleet* *Black Beauty* *Gulliver's Travels* *20,000 Leagues Under the Sea* *The Lost World* *David Copperfield*	**Fiction** *The Powder Monkey* (18th Century) **Fiction More Stories A** *The Worst of the Vikings* **Graphic Novels** *A United Force* (Romans) *Beware of the Vikings* *Gladiator* (Romans) *Master Leonardo* (Renaissance)	**Fiction** *Paradise High* **Fiction More Stories A** *Aliens at Paradise High* *Luke Lively and the Castle of Sleep*	**Graphic Novels** *Lion of Africa* (Africa) *Riches of the Amazon* (Amazon rainforest)
Key Stage 2 Book Band: Year 6, Red **Best fit National Curriculum in England Level: 4/5** **National Curriculum for Wales Level: 4/5** **Northern Ireland Curriculum Level: 4/5**	**Fiction** *In the Shadow of the Striker* *Carnival* **Fiction More Stories A** *One Girl School* *The Multi-Million-Pound Mascot* *Lolly Woe*	**Fiction** *Sister Ella* (retelling of Cinderella) **Myths and Legends** *Tales of the Underworld* *Shapeshifters* *The Legend of Gilgamesh*	**Fiction** *Swivel-Head* **Fiction More Stories A** *Snowblind* **Classics Pack A** *Frankenstein* *Jane Eyre* *Sherlock Holmes* *Wuthering Heights* *Treasure Island* *Robinson Crusoe* **Classics Pack B** *The Tempest* *Oliver Twist* *Silas Marner* *Kidnapped* *Dr Jekyll and Mr Hyde* *Macbeth*	**Fiction More Stories A** *The War Monkey* (Second World War) **Graphic Novels** *Code Talkers* (Second World War) *Fight for Rights* (Victorian/Edwardian) *Freedom Train* (19th Century) *Queen Nzinga* (17th Century) *The Hidden Message* (Tudor)	**Fiction** *Melleron's Monsters* *Melleron's Magic* **Fiction More Stories A** *Rat Squad*	**Graphic Novels** *The Caged Bird* (Burma)

Stage 15

Stage 16

Non-fiction overview (including Book Bands and Curriculum Levels)

The chart that follows shows the Key Stage 2 Book Band and National Curriculum Levels for each Stage of TreeTops non-fiction, plus curriculum correlation information for Northern Ireland and Wales. It also shows the subject matter and lists the text type of each non-fiction title, to help you select the most appropriate books for your children's needs. TreeTops non-fiction offers examples of the following non-fiction text types: explanations, instructions, chronological recounts, non-chronological reports, examples of persuasive writing, biography and autobiography, discussion texts and alphabetical texts.

Book Band / Curriculum Level in England, Wales and Northern Ireland	Science	Arts	Geography	History	Sport	Other subjects
Stage 9 — **Key Stage 2 Book Band:** Year 3, Brown / **Best fit National Curriculum in England Level: 2** / **National Curriculum for Wales Level: 2** / **Northern Ireland Curriculum Level: 2**	**Non-fiction** / *Did You Know That ...?* (information text) / *Further, Faster, Higher* (travel; information text)	**Non-fiction** / *Picture This!* (instruction/information text)		**Non-fiction** / *Visual Vikings* (alphabetical text)		**Non-fiction** / *Against All Odds* (PHSE/Citizenship; information text) / *What in the World are Fairies?* (non-chronological report)
Stage 10 — **Key Stage 2 Book Band:** Year 3, Brown / **Best fit National Curriculum in England Level: 2** / **National Curriculum for Wales Level: 2** / **Northern Ireland Curriculum Level: 2**	**Non-fiction** / *How to Make Soil* (instructions/explanation text) / *The Power of Plants* (non-chronological report) / *Cleared for Take-off!* (recount/information text) / **Non-fiction Pack A** / *Amazing Brain* (non-chronological report) / *Animal Parents* (non-chronological report) / *Seeing the Stars* (non-chronological report)	**Non-fiction** / *Amazing Paint!* (explanation text/information text)		**Non-fiction** / *Edward and Tom Prince and Pauper* (Tudors; historical report/recount) / **Non-fiction Pack A** / *Horrid Heroes and Magic Monsters* (Ancient Greece; historical report) / **True Stories Pack 1** / *My Friend, Mandela* (biography) / *The Mystery of the Cocos Gold* (historical recount)	**Non-fiction** / *Sport is Fun!* (non-chronological report)	**Non-fiction Pack A** / *The Fame Game* (PHSE/Citizenship; celebrity culture; information/discussion text) / *It's Magic!* (PHSE/Citizenship; learning about jobs; report/instructions)

© Oxford University Press: 2010

Copying permitted within purchasing school only

Book Band Curriculum Level in England, Wales and Northern Ireland	Science	Arts	Geography	History	Sport	Other subjects
Key Stage 2 Book Band: Year 3, Brown **Best fit National Curriculum in England Level: 2/3** **National Curriculum for Wales Level: 2/3** **Northern Ireland Curriculum Level: 2/3** **Stage 11**	**Non-fiction** *Cutters and Crushers* (animal teeth; non-chronological report) **Non-fiction Pack A** *Lost and Found* (discovered and extinct animal species; non-chronological report) *What is Time?* (explanation text) *Monsters from the Deep* (non-chronological report)			**Non-fiction** *Wall Soldier* (Romans; historical recount) *The Tower of London* (Tudors; historical report/recount) *War Children* (Second World War; historical recount/report) *Picture Dictionary of Ancient Egypt* (alphabetical text) **Non-fiction Pack A** *Stages through the Ages* (history of theatre; historical report/recount) *A Guide to Revolting Rome* (historical report/recount) *Great Blunders* (historical report/recount) **True Stories Pack 1** *Sea Empress Disaster* (recount)		**Non-fiction** *A–Z of Survival* (PHSE/Citizenship; alphabetical text)
Key Stage 2 Book Band: Year 4, Grey **Best fit National Curriculum in England Level: 3/4** **National Curriculum for Wales Level: 3/4** **Northern Ireland Curriculum Level: 3/4** **Stage 12**	**Non-fiction** *What Can You See in this Cloud?* (information text) *The Flick of a Switch* (explanation text) **Non-fiction Pack A** *It's Chaos!* (non-chronological report) *To Infinity and Beyond!* (stories of journeys of exploration; report/recount)	**Non-fiction Pack A** *Moving Pictures* (animated films; information text/explanation text) **True Stories Pack 1** *Over the Rainbow* (biography of Judy Garland)	**True Stories Pack 1** *Fayim's Incredible Journey* (recount set in Afghanistan)	**Non-fiction** *What's Strange About Saturday?* (history of names of days of the week; report) **Non-fiction Pack A** *And so to Bed...* (non-chronological report) *Celebrating Black History* (historical report/recount)	**True Stories Pack 1** *Cup Winners* (recount)	**Non-fiction** *Do Monsters Exist?* (information/discussion text) *Breaking News: Shipwreck!* (recount/explanation text) *Let's Look at Adverts* (information text/persuasive text) **Non-fiction Pack A** *The Unexplained* (UFOs; non-chronological report)

Book Band / Curriculum Level in England, Wales and Northern Ireland	Science	Arts	Geography	History	Sport	Other subjects
Stage 13 — **Key Stage 2 Book Band:** Year 4, Grey Band; Year 5, Blue **Best fit National Curriculum Level: 3/4** **National Curriculum for Wales Level: 3/4** **Northern Ireland Curriculum Level: 3/4**		**Non-fiction** *Wonderful Things* (information text) *Making Music* (report/recount) **True Stories Pack 2** *This is Me! Mel B!* (biography of a singer)	**Non-fiction** *Save Our Coasts!* (non-chronological report/explanation text) *Under the Volcano* (explanation text/historical recount)	**Non-fiction** *Hard Work* (working children in Victorian times; historical recount) **True Stories Pack 2** *Blackbeard's Last Stand* (recount)		**Non-fiction** *Winning Words* (word derivations and their meanings; non-chronological report) **True Stories Pack 2** *Kelly the Rescue Dog* (recount)
Stage 14 — **Key Stage 2 Book Band:** Year 5, Blue **Best fit National Curriculum in England Level: 3/4** **National Curriculum for Wales Level: 3/4** **Northern Ireland Curriculum Level: 3/4**	**Non-fiction** *Animals and Us* (argument/discussion text) *The Moon* (non-chronological report) **True Stories Pack 2** *Race Against Time* (Apollo 13 mission; recount)		**Non-fiction** *Maps, Measurements and Meanings* (explanation text) *The Power of Nature* (weather; non-chronological report/explanation text) **True Stories Pack 2** *Antarctic Adventure* (recount)	**Non-fiction** *Write Now* (letters from different times in history; recounts) **True Stories Pack 2** *Tomb Raiders* (discovery of Tutankhamun's tomb; historical recount)		**Non-fiction** *How to Shock Your Parents* (PHSE/Citizenship: respecting the differences between people; historical report/recount)

© Oxford University Press: 2010

Copying permitted within purchasing school only

Book Band / Curriculum Level in England, Wales and Northern Ireland	Science	Arts	Geography	History	Sport	Other subjects
Stage 15 **Key Stage 2 Book Band:** Year 6, Red **Best fit National Curriculum in England Level: 4/5** **National Curriculum for Wales Level: 4/5** **Northern Ireland Curriculum Level: 4/5**	**Non-fiction** *Robots – Friend or Foe?* (non-chronological report/ discussion text) *Eyes of Every Shape and Size* (non-chronological report)	**Non-fiction** *Michael Rosen's Scrapbook* (information text about the poet and how he works) **True Stories Pack 3** *Carnival King* (biography of the musician Cartola)		**Non-fiction** *What's Left Behind?* (historical evidence; non-chronological report) *Pirates* (non-chronological report/recount) **True Stories Pack 3** *Black Death* (historical recount) *Tomahawk Beckwourth* (historical recount/ biography)		**Non-fiction** *Reach for the Skies* (PHSE/Citizenship; overcoming disabilities; recounts)
Stage 16 **Key Stage 2 Book Band:** Year 6, Red **Best fit National Curriculum in England Level: 4/5** **National Curriculum for Wales Level: 4/5** **Northern Ireland Curriculum Level: 4/5**	**Non-fiction** *Explosions* (properties of materials; non-chronological report) *Pests, Plagues and Parasites* (non-chronological report) *Our Earth is Unique* (persuasive text/non-chronological report) *Let's Go to the Planets!* (non-chronological report) *Planet Granite* (rocks; non-chronological report)			**Non-fiction** *Arms and Armour* (non-chronological report) **True Stories Pack 3** *I Runned Away to Sea* (Victorian times; first person historical recount) *Whitemen* (Australia in the mid-19th Century; historical recount)		**True Stories Pack 3** *Threads of Deceit* (PHSE/ Citizenship: the Indian carpet industry and modern slavery; recount)

TreeTops and Key Stage 1 Book Bands

The charts on pages 85 to 93 show how each Stage of TreeTops corresponds to the Key Stage 2 Book Bands. However, some of the TreeTops books were also included in *Book Bands for Guided Reading* and *Bridging Bands for Guided Reading* which show the Key Stage 1 Book Bands. The chart below shows those Key Stage 1 Book Bands. If a book is not mentioned in this chart, it does not appear in *Book Bands for Guided Reading* or *Bridging Bands for Guided Reading*.

Series and stage	Book title	Key Stage 1 Book Band
TreeTops Fiction Stage 9	Captain Comet and the Purple Planet	Gold
	Messy Ella	Gold
	Robo-Vac	Gold
	The Big Little Dinosaur	Gold
	The Spooks	Gold
	Noisy Neighbours	Gold
TreeTops Fiction Stage 9 More Stories A	Captain Comet and the Dog Star	Gold
	Bigboots the Spider	Gold
	Princess Pip's Holiday	Gold
	Oh, Otto!	Gold
	The Cowboy Next Door	Gold
	Walrus Joins In	Gold
TreeTops Fiction Stage 10	Jungle Shorts	Purple
	The Squink	Purple
	Mr Stofflees and the Painted Tiger	Gold
	The Boss Dog of Blossom Street	Gold
	The Masked Cleaning Ladies of Om	Gold
	The Masked Cleaning Ladies Save the Day	Gold
TreeTops Fiction Stage 10 More Stories A	Purple Buttons	Gold
	The Great Spaghetti Suit	Gold
	Stupid Trousers	Gold
	The Masked Cleaning Ladies Meet the Pirates	Gold
	Dexter's Dinosaurs	Gold
	Jellyfish Shoes	Gold
TreeTops Fiction Stage 10 More Stories B	Dustbin	White
	The Ghost Ship	White
	Cornflake Coin	White
	Fast Frog	White
	Micro the Metal Dog	White
	Half Price Hero	White
TreeTops Playscripts Stage 10	The Masked Cleaning Ladies of Om	Gold
	Stupid Trousers	Gold
TreeTops True Stories Pack 1	My Friend Mandela	White
	The Mystery of Cocos Gold	White

© Oxford University Press: 2010   Copying permitted within purchasing school only

Series and stage	Book title	Key Stage 1 Book Band
TreeTops Fiction Stage 11	Flans Across the River	Gold
	Amy the Hedgehog Girl	White
	Bertha's Secret Battle	White
	Bertie Wiggins' Amazing Ears	White
	Coming Clean	White
	Hard to Please	White
TreeTops Fiction Stage 11 More Stories A	The Wrong Letter	Gold
	Blackbones Saves the School	White
	The Big Chance	Lime
	Janey's Giants	Lime
	An Odd Job for Bob and Benny	Lime
	Dangerous Trainers	Lime
TreeTops Fiction Stage 11 More Stories B	The Luckless Monster	Lime
	Stinky Street	Lime
	The Fabulous Food Machine	Lime
	My Dad Does Belly Dancing	Lime
	Jem Stone Genie and the Crash	Lime
	Robot Childminder	Lime
TreeTops Playscripts Stage 11	Bertie Wiggins' Amazing Ears	White
	Bertha's Secret Battle	White
TreeTops True Stories Pack 1	Fayim's Incredible Journey	White
	Over the Rainbow	White
	Cup Winners	Lime
	Sea Empress Disaster	Lime
TreeTops Fiction Stage 12	Hamper's Great Escape	Gold
	Cool Clive	Lime
	Clive Keeps his Cool	Lime
	Robbie Woods and his Merry Men	Lime
	Scrapman	Lime
	The Lie Detector	Lime
TreeTops Fiction Stage 12 More Stories A	Cool Clive and the Little Pest	Lime
	Here Comes Trouble	Lime
	Pass the Ball!	Lime
	Shelly Holmes Ace Detective	Lime
	Snooty Prune	Lime
	Billy's Luck	Lime
TreeTops Fiction Stage 12 More Stories B	Dads Win Prizes	Lime
	Doohickey and the Robot	Lime
	A Kitten in Daisy Street	Lime
	Kid Wonder and the Terrible Truth	Lime
	Me and my Newt	Lime
	Scrapman and Scrapcat	Lime
TreeTops Fiction Stage 12 More Stories C	Cool Clive and the Bubble Trouble	White
	Shelly Holmes, Animal Trainer	White
	Kid Wonder and the Sticky Skyscraper	Lime
	Doughnut Dilemma	Lime
	Kid Wonder and the Half-Hearted Hero	Lime
	Scrapman and the Incredible Flying Machine	Lime

Series and stage	Book title	Key Stage 1 Book Band
TreeTops Playscripts Stage 12	Blue Shoes	Lime
	The Lie Detector	Lime
TreeTops Fiction Stage 13	I Wish, I Wish	Lime
	The Case of the Smiling Shark	Lime
	The Goalie's Secret	Lime
	The Personality Potion	Lime
	The Ultimate Trainers	Lime
	Waiting for Goldie	Lime
TreeTops Fiction Stage 13 More Stories A	Black Dan	Lime
	Bones	Lime
	Spooky!	Lime
	The Goalie from Nowhere	Lime
	The Monster in the Wardrobe	Lime
	The Revenge of Captain Blood	Lime
TreeTops Fiction Stage 13 More Stories B	The True Diary of Carly Ann Potter	Lime
	The Anti-Bully Machine	Lime
	Cat Out of the Bag	Lime
	The Quest for the Golden See-Saw	Lime
	Star Struck	Lime
	Pet Squad	Lime
TreeTops Playscripts Stage 13	The Personality Potion	Lime
	Spooky!	Lime
TreeTops Non-fiction Stage 13	Save Our Coasts!	Lime
	Hard Work	Lime
	Under the Volcano	Lime
	Wonderful Things	Lime
	Making Music	Lime
	Winning Words	Lime
TreeTops Fiction Stage 14	Danny's Secret Fox	Lime
	The Night of the Ticklers	Lime
	Okay, Spanner, You Win!	Lime

© Oxford University Press: 2010

Copying permitted within purchasing school only

TreeTops and the wider curriculum

TreeTops contains a wide variety of books to help you tackle many of the most popular cross-curricular topics that children study at Key Stage 2.

The charts on pages 85–93 show how the fiction and non-fiction books in TreeTops can support work in a range of topics across different curriculum areas, including History, Science, Geography and the arts.

In the following pages, you will find links to cross-curricular topics which have been picked out as examples to show how TreeTops can help you to resource topic work. You will find that TreeTops resources can also support a wide range of other topics, and the non-fiction overview chart on pages 90–93 is a good place to start when looking for other ideas for topic work.

In addition, cross-curricular links have been picked out in more detail in the *Teaching Notes* for each pack of books.

Cross-curricular links

TreeTops Non-Fiction More Stage 11A	Cross-curricular link	Other *TreeTops* titles with similar link
Stages through the Ages	**History: British history: 8a:** Britain and the wider world in Tudor times; Victorian Britain and Britain since 1930	*Edward and Tom: Prince and Pauper* (Non-Fiction Stage 10) *The Tower of London* (Non-Fiction Stage 11) *To Infinity and Beyond!* (Non-Fiction More Stage 12A)
Lost and Found	**Science 2: Life processes and living things: 5:** Living things in their environment	*Monsters from the Deep*
A Guide to Revolting Rome	**History: 8a: British history** The Romans, Anglo-Saxons and Vikings	*Wall Soldier* (Non-Fiction Stage 11) *To Infinity and Beyond!* (Non-Fiction More Stage 12A)
Great Blunders	**History: Knowledge and understanding of events, people and changes in the past: 2c:** Identify and describe reasons for, and results of, historical events, situations, and changes in the periods studied	*The Flick of a Switch* (Non-Fiction Stage 12)
What is Time?	**Science 4: Physical processes:** The Earth and beyond	*Seeing the Stars* (Non-Fiction More Stage 10A)
Monsters from the Deep	**Science 2: Life processes and living things:** Living things in their environment	*Lost and Found*

This chart is taken from More Stage 11A *Non-fiction Teaching Notes* and shows the cross-curricular links that can be made with the books at that stage.

Stages 9–11

Roman Britain

Wall Soldier
(about the life of a soldier on Hadrian's Wall)
Stage 11 *Non-fiction*

A Guide to Revolting Rome
(fun facts about Romans and
their way of life)
Stage 11 Pack A *Non-fiction*

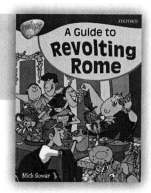

Gods of Thunder
(contains a story about
the Roman god Vulcan)
Stage 10 *Myths and Legends*

You can also use
Oxford Connections
Roman Britain

Teeth and eating

Cutters and Crushers
(about different types of
animal teeth)
Stage 11 *Non-fiction*

Dustbin
(about a dog who loves eating)
Stage 10 More Stories B *Fiction*

The Fabulous Food Machine
(about a machine that its owners
pretend can make wonderful food;
brings in ideas about what really
makes food delicious)
Stage 11 More Stories B *Fiction*

Stages 12–13

Children in history

A Kitten in Daisy Street (about life in a poor Victorian family) Stage 12 More Stories B *Fiction*

Cave of Secrets (about children in prehistoric times) Stage 13 *Graphic Novels*

Hollywood Here I Come (about life for a child in 1920s Hollywood) Stage 13 *Graphic Novels*

The Golden Scarab (set in Ancient Egypt) Stage 13 *Graphic Novels*

Celebrating Black History (including life for black children in the past) Stage 12 Pack A *Non-fiction*

Hard Work (about working children in history) Stage 13 *Non-fiction*

You can also use Oxford Connections *Children in World War 2*

Improving the environment

Me and my Newt (a boy finds a newt in a polluted pond – cleans up the pond and looks after the newt) Stage 12 More Stories B *Fiction*

Save Our Coasts! (about preserving coastal environments) Stage 13 *Non-fiction*

How Winter Came into the World (looks at how the seasons came about from a mythological angle) Stage 13 *Myths and Legends*

Why the Sea is Salty (contains stories with a water theme from a mythological angle) Stage 13 *Myths and Legends*

You can also use Oxford Connections *Improving the Environment* and *Interdependence and Adaptation*

Stages 13–14

Victorians

Climbing in the Dark (about working children in Victorian times) Stage 14 *Fiction*

The Secret Garden (version of the classic novel set in Victorian times) Stage 14 *Classics*

 *Five Children and It* (version of the classic novel set in Victorian/ Edwardian times) Stage 14 *Classics*

 *Hard Work* (includes information about work in Victorian times) Stage 13 *Non-fiction*

You can also use
Oxford Connections *Victorian Children*

Water

Save Our Coasts! (about coastal regions and the coastal environment) Stage 13 *Non-fiction*

The Power of Nature (about the weather) Stage 14 *Non-Fiction*

 *Why the Sea is Salty* (contains stories with water as their theme) Stage 13 *Myths and Legends*

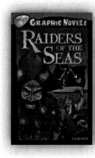 *Raiders of the Seas* (about pirates in the 18th Century) Stage 13 *Graphic Novels*

Sing for your Supper (about child sailors in the 18th/19th Century) Stage 14 More Stories A *Fiction*

You can also use
Oxford Connections
Water and Rivers

Stages 15–16

The Second World War

The War Monkey (set in London during the Second World War)
Stage 16 More Stories A *Fiction*

Code Talkers (about Navajo brothers who help decipher secret messages in the Second World War)
Stage 16 *Graphic Novels*

You can also use
Oxford Connections
Children in World War 2

Ancient Greece

What's Left Behind? (report about understanding historical evidence)
Stage 15 *Non-fiction*

Mythical Beasts and Fabulous Monsters (stories about mythical creatures)
Stage 15 *Myths and Legends*

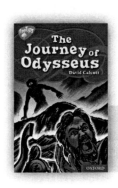

The Journey of Odysseus (a retelling of the classic Ancient Greek myth)
Stage 15 *Myths and Legends*

Tales of the Underworld (contains the Ancient Greek myth of Orpheus and Eurydice)
Stage 16 *Myths and Legends*

You can also use
Oxford Connections
The Greeks

Photocopy masters

The photocopy masters (PCMs) in this section provide a bank of planning tools and activities to help children get to grips with reading, writing and general literacy activities using the TreeTops books. You can use the PCMs with any of the TreeTops books.

Reading PCMs

- **Talking about books: Fiction** (pages 103 and 104) are aimed at teachers and provide generic question prompts and ideas that can be used to help children think and talk about any fiction book. You can use these questions to structure a book conversation with an individual child or a reading group.

- **Talking about books: Non-fiction** (pages 105 and 106) are also aimed at teachers and give a similar list of generic questions to encourage children to explore and think about any non-fiction book.

- **Story mountain** (page 107) provides a framework for children to use to make notes on the plot of a story they have read. The 'story mountain' plot structure works for most simple fiction and can also be used to help children plan their own stories.

- **Emotions graph** (pages 108 and 109) is a two-page PCM that shows how an emotions graph can be used to plot a character's emotional journey throughout a story. The first page provides children with an example in the context of a well known story (Cinderella) and the second page is a blank graph for children to plot the main character's emotions in any story they have read.

Writing PCMs

- **Helping hand: planning** (page 110) provides a simple planning framework that works with most kinds of fiction writing. Children can use it to help plan their stories.

- **Settings planner** (page 111) helps children to think about the structure of a story by focusing on the different settings.

- **Chronological recount planner** (page 112) is a blank timeline which can be used to help children structure biographical recounts and other chronologically structured texts (including fiction as well as non-fiction).

- **Instruction and explanation text planner** (page 113) is a flow chart with prompts to help children create their own sequential instruction and explanation texts.

- **Non-chronological report planner** (page 114) can be used to help plan a simple, short non-chronological report text. For a longer text, children could use one of these sheets for each section.

- **Discussion and argument text planner** (page 115) is structured to help children think through their arguments in a discussion text.

Literacy activity PCMs

- **Word sort** (pages 116 and 117) provides a framework for a range of activities in which children identify and sort words with different functions. This will help to enhance their vocabulary and knowledge of grammar. The first page provides teachers with instructions on how to use the PCM with children in a variety of ways.

- **Powerful words** (pages 118, 119 and 120) can be used to help capture effective word choices across a range of texts.

Here are some open questions which you can adapt to help children think and talk about any fiction book. Use the questions as a starting point and encourage children to add their own ideas and to raise further questions that they may have about the text. Most of the questions below can be used either during children's reading or when they have finished the book. However, some of the *Predicting* questions can be used before children start to read.

Predicting

Before reading

- What do you think this story will be about?
- Where and when is it set?
- Who do you think the book is written for?
- What kind of story do you think it will be? (e.g. funny, sad, realistic, fantasy, etc.)
- Can you get any clues about the type of story from the first paragraph?

During reading

- What would happen if character X was not in the story?
- What would you do now if you were the main character?
- What clues are in the text to suggest that X could happen?
- What do you think will happen to the characters next?
- Can you find some evidence in the story to back up your predictions?

Questioning and clarifying

- What is unusual about the story?
- What would you like to know about the main character?
- Tell me more about the setting of the story.
- How would you describe the dilemma?
- Tell me more about the tense parts of the story.
- How do you think the author creates tension in the story?
- What would you like to ask the author?
- Why do you think the author has described X in this way?
- Use information/evidence from the story to explain why you think that.
- Good writers make careful word choices. Which verbs do you think give us an exact image of how something is happening?
- How do the different characters help each other?
- Why do you think X has happened?
- Do you think the author is being fair to all the characters?
- Can you find any clues in the story to help you work out why X acted like that? After reading the story, create a list of questions you would like one of the characters to answer.

Imagining

- Use information from the story to draw a character or setting.

- Imagine you are one of the minor characters – tell the story from your point of view.

- Write a short diary entry of an important event in the story from a character's point of view.

- Collect words to describe the sensations a character might feel as they travel: what might they hear, see, feel and smell?

- Use a story map to show the main character's life so far, and write additional information on it about the people they have met and how they have treated them.

- How would it feel to arrive in a totally new place? Write a quick diary entry of X's first impressions.

- Imagine you are in the story setting at night – describe or draw what you can hear, feel and see.

- What other examples of characters like X can you think of in other books you have read?

- How would it be different if the main character were a girl/boy?

Summarising

- Look at the opening, and give three reasons why it is successful or not.

- What do we know about the main characters at the end of the first chapter?

- What is the problem in this story?

- Who has the problem?

- How are the characters unusual?

- What would you say are the main themes of the book?

- Can you explain how the author makes the characters change over time?

- Is there evidence to show that some of the characters in the book were misunderstood?

- What would you say is the most important idea in the book so far?

- What do you think is the most powerful image in the text?

- Tell me which part of the text you found the most exciting.

- What surprised you most?

- Compare two characters in the story. How are they similar and how are they different?

- Use a graph to show how a character's feelings change over the course of a story. (See **PCMs 4a and 4b: Emotions graph**).

- Write a blurb for the book.

- Use a timeline to show what happens in the book. (See **PCM 7: Chronological recount planner**).

© Oxford University Press: 2010   Copying permitted within purchasing school only

Here are some open questions which you can adapt to help children think and talk about any non-fiction book. Use the questions as a starting point and encourage children to add their own ideas and to raise further questions that they may have about the text. Most of the questions below can be used either during children's reading or when they have finished the book. However, some of the *Predicting* questions can be used before children start to read.

Predicting

Before reading

- What subject do you think this book is about?
- What do you already know about this subject? What would you like to find out more about?
- Why do you think the author wrote this book?
- Who might find this information useful?

During reading

- Looking at the heading and pictures. What do you think this section will be about?
- Where in the book would you look for information on X? What can you use to help you find this information?
- Can you think of any extra information that might help someone who wants to do this experiment/follow these instructions/find out about this subject?

Questioning and clarifying

- Does it matter in which order you read this text?
- Why do you think the author included this piece of information here?
- Did anything puzzle you about this book/section?
- Can you identify what type of text this is? How do you know? What evidence can you find to back this up?
- Is there any technical language that you need to check the meaning of?
- How do the sub-headings help us when we are reading?
- Can you replace one of the sub-headings with one of your own?
- Why does the author use pictures and captions?

Imagining

- How else could you organise this text?
- Can you draw a diagram to sum up what the text tells us about X?
- Can you show the information on X in the form of a mind map?
- How could you use the information in this book?
- What could you do to the text to make it easier to read?

Summarising

- What is the main subject of the text?
- What do you think is the purpose of this text?
- What is the key message? Sum it up in three sentences.
- Are some ideas in the text more important than others? Which are the most important ones?
- Has reading the text changed your opinion? How?
- What do you think the author's point of view is?
- Can you identify any techniques the author uses to get you to agree with them?
- Choose one paragraph and try to make as short a sentence as possible, summing up what it says.
- How could you adapt the information in this book/section for a younger audience?

© Oxford University Press: 2010

Copying permitted within purchasing school only

Name .... Date ....

Use the story mountain to help you make notes on the plot of a story that you have read.

Title of story ....

Main problem
Something exciting happens!
What is it? What do the characters do?

Suspense!
Does something go wrong
before the problem is solved?

Build-up
A small problem happens.

Solution
How is the problem solved?
What do the characters learn?
How does the story end?

Introduction
Who is the story about?
Where is it set?

Extra idea! You could use the story mountain to plan your own story.

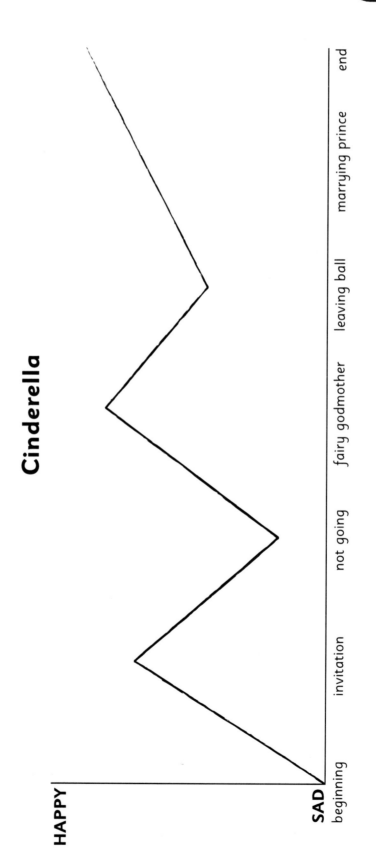
Name .... Date ....

The emotions graph shows how a character's feelings change throughout a story. When the character is feeling happy, the line goes upwards; when the character is sad, it drops downwards. The completed graph shows how a character's feelings change as the story progresses.

Here you can see that Cinderella was sad at the beginning of the story, happy when the invitation to the ball arrived, but became sad when she heard that she would not be allowed to go. Then the Fairy Godmother makes her wishes come true, but she has to leave the ball early. Finally, she is very happy when she marries the Prince.

Cinderella

HAPPY

SAD

beginning   invitation   not going   fairy godmother   leaving ball   marrying prince   end

PCM 4b: Emotions graph, provides a blank emotions graph for you to use to show how one character's emotions change in a story you have read.

Name .... Date ....

Choose a character from a book you have read, and use the blank emotions graph below to show how their feelings changed throughout the book. For instructions on filling in the graph, (see **PCM 4a: Emotions graph**).

Story: ....

Character: ....

HAPPY

SAD

beginning

end

Extra idea! You could use the completed graph to create a new story in which the main character's feelings follow a similar pattern.

Copying permitted within purchasing school only

Name .... Date ....

Use the diagram below to help plan your own story.

Who is the story about?

Where is the story set?

What is the problem/main event?

How is the problem solved?

How does the story end?

Extra idea!
You could also use the hand diagram to help you to summarise the main events of a story that you have read.

© Oxford University Press: 2010 Copying permitted within purchasing school only

Settings planner

TreeTops

Name .... Date ....

Where does your story start? Where does the action go to next?
Where does it finish?

Make a note of the different settings and what happens in each.

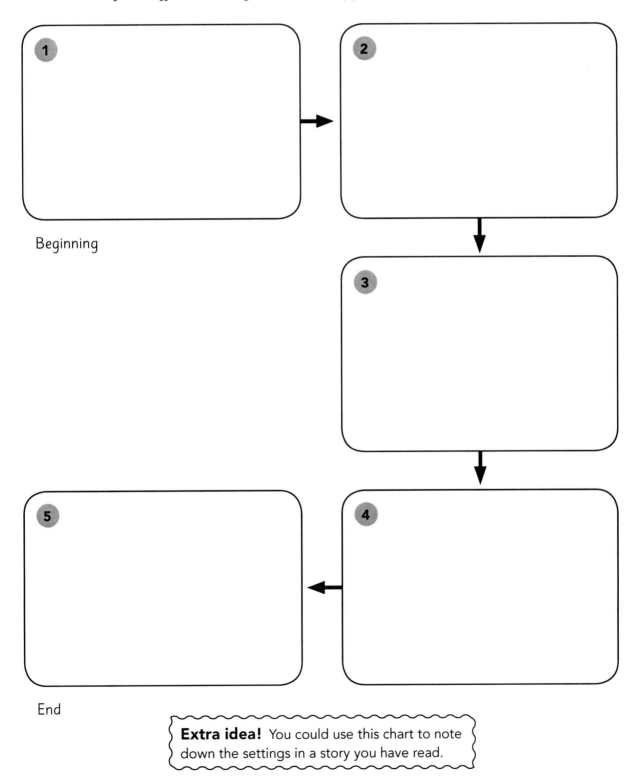

1

2

Beginning

3

5

4

End

Extra idea! You could use this chart to note
down the settings in a story you have read.

Chronological recount planner

TreeTops

Name .... Date ....

You can use this planner to help you write any text that follows a chronological order, e.g. a biography, diary, non-fiction recount or story.

Write events in the flags. Write the time/date, or order of events in the boxes along the bottom.

© Oxford University Press: 2010

Copying permitted within purchasing school only

Name .... Date ....

Use these boxes to help you plan an instruction or explanation text. If you need more stages in your instructions or explanation, add another sheet.

Questions to think about:

What are you giving instructions for or explaining?

What ingredients or equipment are needed?

What are the steps in the process?

What should the outcome be?

© Oxford University Press: 2010

Copying permitted within purchasing school only

Non-chronological report planner

Name .... Date ....

Use this diagram to help you plan non-chronological reports or information texts on any subject.

Write your subject heading in the big circle and add sub-headings in the smaller circles.

Add lines from each sub-heading to show the key words connected to them. Use a coloured pen to highlight any technical language, you may need to write a glossary for these words if their meaning is not clear.

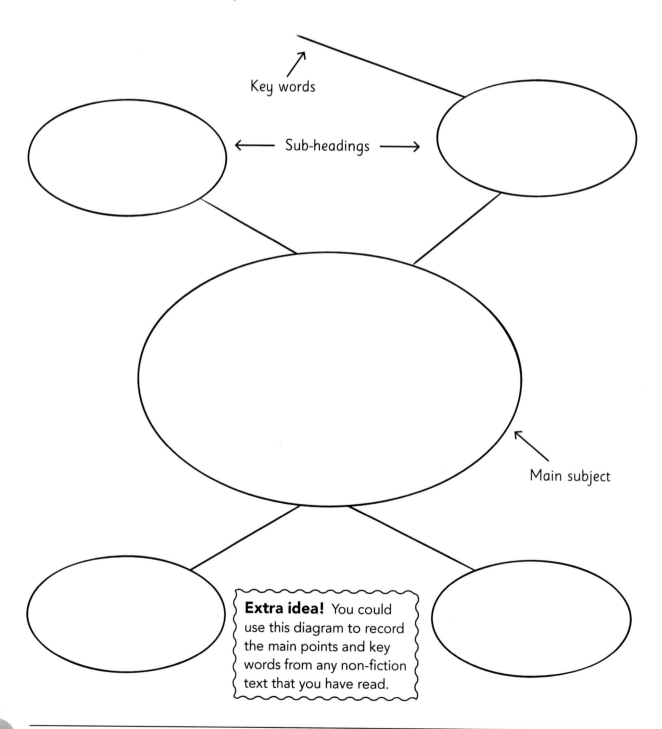

Key words

Sub-headings

Main subject

Extra idea! You could use this diagram to record the main points and key words from any non-fiction text that you have read.

© Oxford University Press: 2010

Copying permitted within purchasing school only

Name .... Date ....

Use this to plan a discussion or argument. Record the main ideas for and against the subject. Keep a note of any persuasive words, phrases, facts and opinions.

The subject to be discussed

| |
| |

Ideas for	**Ideas against**	**Persuasive words**

What you think at the end

| |
| |

Word sort

The PCM to follow – **PCM11b: Word sort** – can be used in several ways:

1. Ask the children to choose words from their book to place in the right category, for example, using page 12 of *War Children* (Stage 11 *Non-fiction*):

Noun	Verb	Adjective	Adverb
men	joined	young	anxiously

2. Cut the sheet into vertical strips and ask different children to look in the book for examples of one part of speech and to create a list.

3. Write a word in one column that can be changed to create different parts of speech. For example, write *memory* in the 'Noun' box and discuss how to spell words for the other parts of speech:

Noun	Verb	Adjective	Adverb
memory	memorise	memorable	memorably

© Oxford University Press: 2010

Copying permitted within purchasing school only

Word sort

Noun	Verb	Adjective	Adverb

© Oxford University Press: 2010

Name .... Date ....

As you read, collect words that can be used instead of 'said' or 'thought'.
Write one word in each speech bubble or thought cloud.

yelled

wondered

© Oxford University Press: 2010

Copying permitted within purchasing school only

TreeTops

Powerful words for sounds

Pupils'
sheet

**PCM
12b**

Literacy

Name .... Date ....

As you read, collect words that can be used to describe sounds. Write one
word in each shape.

Loud words

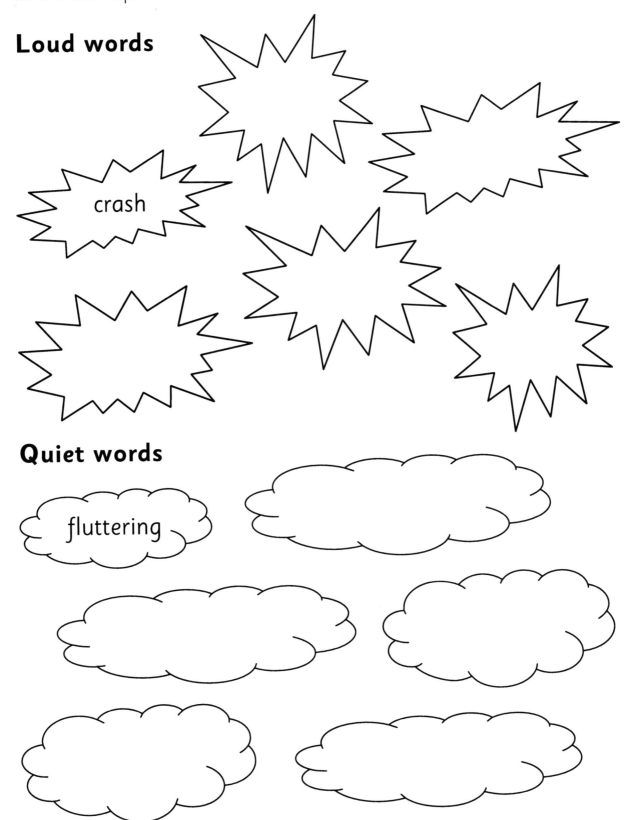

crash

Quiet words

fluttering

© Oxford University Press: 2010

Name .... Date ....

As you read, collect words that can be used to describe ways of moving.
Write one word in each shape.

On foot

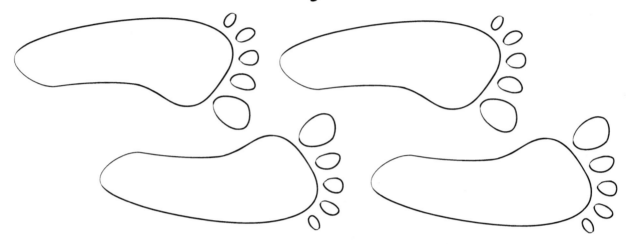

In a vehicle

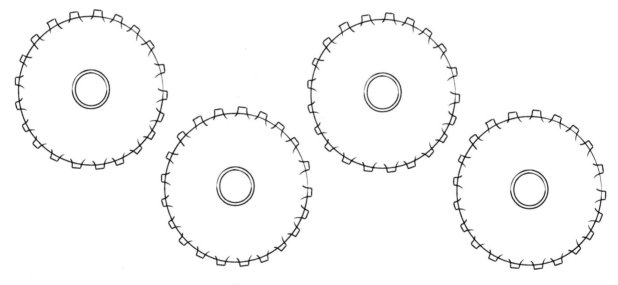

On horseback

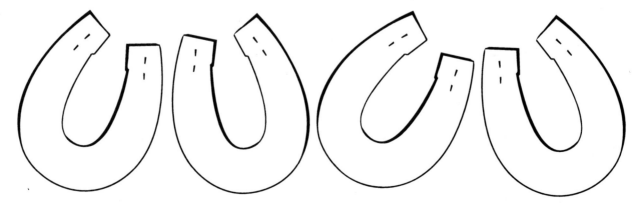

© Oxford University Press: 2010

Copying permitted within purchasing school only